Front Cover Photo: Ancestors of Author or some of her extended family making their way westward by covered wagons being ferried over a swollen river, eventually settling in Otero County, at that time, New Mexico Territory. Circa 1885. Courtesy of Marjorie 'Dockray' Curtis

Pioneer Settlers of New Mexico Territory

The Journeys of a Tough and Resilient People

by

Deloris Kay Curtis-Ward

authorHOUSE®

AuthorHouse™
1663 Liberty Drive, Suite 200
Bloomington, IN 47403
www.authorhouse.com
Phone: 1-800-839-8640

First published by AuthorHouse 11/24/2008

ISBN: 978-1-4389-0043-8 (sc)

Printed in the United States of America
Bloomington, Indiana

This book is printed on acid-free paper.

Author, Deloris Kay 'Curtis' Ward

This depicts the Authors life!
Drug Problem

I HAD A "DRUG" PROBLEM WHEN I WAS A YOUNG
PERSON AND TEENAGER:

I was "drug" to Sunday School every Sunday Morning

I was "drug" to Worship Services every Sunday Morning

I was "drug" to Worship Services every Sunday Night

I was "drug" to Bible Study every Wednesday Night

I was "drug" to Vacation Bible School every Summer

I was "drug" to the family gathering to read the Bible and pray.

I was "drug" to the woodshed when I disobeyed my Parent's.

Those "drugs" are still in my veins; and they affect my

Behavior in ever thing I do, say and think. They are

stronger than cocaine, crack or heroin. If your children had

this kind of "drug" problem, wouldn't America be a better

place for everyone?

THANKS TO MY MOM, DAD AND GRANDMOTHER!

*Author Unknown

Via The Good News

Church of Christ, Elgin, Texas

Dedication

I am dedicating this book to all my family that encouraged me and shared information with me. Thank you so much for loving and believing in me.

A special thank you to my sister Louise Honeycutt for supporting me in this endeavor and for reading and rereading to edit for me.

A very special thanks to Marilyn McMurry, that I deeply love like a sister, that helped and put a lot of time on research.

Also to Dale Dawson for the gift of the J.B. Dawson book and for looking over and editing for me.

For the family of Aunt Naomia that so generously gave me information and that worked near to thirty years to find our historical past.

To Melvin Brashears for his work on finding our relatives back to England.

To Preston and his wife Jeanne Brantley who so diligently researched the Brantley family (*and in his memory*) with love. He was born October 2, 1928 and Passed away on December 26, 2006.

For all the other Curtis and Brantley families that shared their information. To L.A. Curtis that was so looking forward to the finished book. (*In Memory of him*) with love. He passed away before getting to read it. Born Loyd Alton Curtis Jr. in Mayhill, N.M. on September 5, 1930 and passed from this life on March 6, 2008 in Hot Spring, AR.

Introduction

This work has been done so the next generations will know about their family history and how our True Pioneer Heritage made the United States the greatest country there is to live in.

Men like my Great Grandfathers, Joel Warner Curtis and Fredrick Brantley and their friends that they traveled with, lived around and intermarried with.

Joel Warner Curtis fought in the Mexican War, and was a cattle drover (cowboy). He rode across vast and uninhabited plains and mountains and fought against Indians and Civil War renegades. He traveled thousands of miles within a few short years, on horse back or by an oxen or horse drawn wagon.

He was one of the first of a few men that settled in the Lincoln County Territory, of New Mexico. This land was known for an outlaw by the name of Henry McCarty (alias: William Bonney) but better known as Billy the Kid and a renegade Indian by the name of Geronimo.

Fred Brantley's Father, Josiah Brantley fought in the Blackhawk Indian Wars along with one of his brothers, Henry. Fred and his family came to settle in the Lincoln County Territory some time later than the Curtis's and became well known through out the land as being a fair and honest man. A hard working, God fearing man, and a very good neighbor to everyone.

These people that settled and lived in Lincoln County (later to become Otero County and New Mexico a state of the union) were the rock foundation for all generations to follow. They deserve to be recognized and admired for their service and love of God and fellow man.

Some of The Curtis family, through a lot of years of scraping for information finally traced the Curtis's back to Nazeing, England. The only man that was known of the ancestors was Joel Warner Curtis Jr.. None of the family knew who his parents were much less the ones further back or that he was a Jr..

Joel Warner Curtis Jr. was born on March 10, 1818 in Trumbull County, Ohio, to the 10th child of Ethan and Elizabeth Warner Curtis, Joel Warner Curtis Sr..

Ethan Curtis was born December 3, 1753 in Wallingford, New Haven County, Connecticut. He married Elizabeth Warner, born June 2, 1758, on February 9, 1776. They had 13 children: Lydia, Sarah, Samuel, Ethan A., Chauncey, Elizabeth, Eunice, Adah, John Salter, Joel Warner, Catherine, George Willis, and William Nelson. Ethan died October 29, 1815 in Burlington, Hartford County, Connecticut and Elizabeth Died September 21, 1810 in the same place as Ethan.

Joel Warner Sr. was born April 30, 1796 and married Sally Hulet(Hulett) September 18, 1817. She was born January 2, 1799 in Tyringham, Berkshire County, Massachusetts and was known for her beauty and indiscretions. In the search by one of my cousins, Melvin Brashers, he found records of an adjoining property to Joel and Sally in Medina county, that belonged to Ethan and adjacent property owned by Samuel, his son. Ethan bought the property from William Hulet, Sally's father. Joel and Sally had a son born in Medina County where they continued to reside. The son was born between 1817, their marriage year, and 1820 when daughter Sally was born. This son disappeared from the ensuing family history and He believes that this is our Joel. The deeds of the adjacent properties imply that Joel and Sally were in Medina County. He also found newspaper accounts of the same. The date of their first born son bridge our Joel's birth date. In addition all other offspring are accounted for with the brothers except for Joel and Sally's missing son. He found recorded accounts of Sally's "reputation", so the circumstance of our Joel's birth may account for his secrecy including changing the location of his birthplace and his parents in several U.S. Census surveys.

Joel Sr. died April 6, 1845 in Ohio and Sally died January 26, 1878. They had nine children, Joel Jr. being the first, then Sally, Mary, Hannah, Jane E., Andrew Thomas, Della, Samuel, and Isaac Joel.

At an unknown time Joel Jr. did leave his parents and Ohio, moving westward. No one knows where his wanderings took him, up to 1846. The first knowledge of him, by our generation, was found in a trunk of one of his daughters, Naomai, that revealed his presence in Washington, Arkansas.

According to something that had been told to Zenus Curtis, by someone in his family, Possibly his mother Henrietta Dawson (John Dawson's sister) "Henrietta married Joel W. Curtis from Trigg County Kentucky and they moved to the Vermejo ." This sounds as though Joel wandered into Kentucky, from Ohio, and met the Dawson family and stayed with them as they traveled to Arkansas. This would solve the problem of our wondering how he knew Henrietta and why he married her soon after returning from the Mexican War. He may have joined them because they were moving west and he would have someone to travel with.

In 1810 Mexico rebelled against Spain. In 1821 Mexico won their independence from Spain. During that time France forced Spain to give back the land around Texas called Louisiana. Then France sold that land to the United States in 1803, which became known as the "Louisiana Purchase".

After Mexico won independence they flew the Mexican flag over Texas for fifteen years until 1836. During these years Mexico wanted prosperity in that region but they had hostile Indians roaming free which prevented their people from settling there. Because of this a man from the U.S. named Stephen F. Austin made a deal with Mexico to bring three hundred families from the U.S. to a fertile block of land along the Texas Gulf Coast and inland from there a ways.

There were rules put on them, if they lived there they had to adhere to the Catholic faith and other Mexican ideals. Austin tried to do this and to keep the other folks adhering also but immigrants kept coming in and the Mexican officials started to worry about holding the land, so they started putting restrictions and taxes on them. Austin became upset over this and rebellion broke out.

The people chose a new immigrant, Sam Houston, to lead them. He had been a leader in Tennessee, his native home. Other men, that became famous, also came to help in the rebellion: William Barret Travis, Jim Bowie, Davey Crockett, James Fannin, Daniel Boone and James Bonham.

There were also some Mexicans that fought for the Texas revolt, even they were upset over the man that became dictator of Mexico. His name was Antonio Lopez de Santa Ana. He was a general that had been trained by Spanish officers before Mexico independence. He was a moody, cruel, and savage man and had been crushing rebellions inside Mexico that were turning against his leadership. On February 23, 1836, Santa Ana and his first troops, finally numbered five thousand, arrived in San Antonio.

At this time General Santa Ana closed in on an abandoned Spanish Mission that they called the Alamo, where some two hundred or less had locked themselves into. Barret sent a message for others to come and help but only about thirty two men, from Gonzales, came to help.

The all out attack came in the morning of March 6, 1836 shortly after 5:00 A.M.. One and a half hours and one hundred and eighty three dead defenders later, the Alamo had been taken. The one hundred and eighty three dead were all men who had fought to the end but there were some that survived the battle of the Alamo. A few women and children were left to live and among them one woman, that became well known, and her fifteen month old daughter. The estimated cost of men to Mexico was as high as fifteen hundred.

Two weeks after the Alamo fell Colonel Fannin was trying to move his soldiers east of Goliad, on the orders of General Sam Houston, but they were surrounded and forced to surrender. On March 27th by order of Santa Ana they were executed. Fannin and three hundred and forty two of his men died that day.

Santa Ana and a large army then went in pursuit of Houston. On a low plain which is now called Houston, Santa Ana stopped. On April 21, 1836 in a spot called the San Jacinto battlefield in the afternoon about 3:30 while the Mexican soldiers were having a 'siesta' Houston's angry men, by count of nine hundred and eighteen, rode into their camp. As they entered the camp they started yelling "Remember the Alamo" as they fired their arms and clubbed the soldiers.

Another piece of information was reported by a Billingsley.

With the exception of the following paragraph which has been rearranged this write up of Captain Jesse Billingsley is by E.L. Bilingsley, of Dallas, Texas.

In 1835 Jesse Billingsley migrated to Texas and settled on Cedar Creek in Mina Settlement, later Bastrop County. He organized the Mina Volunteers and was elected Captain. On the 28 February 1836 his company was enrolled as company C, 1st Texas Regiment, commanded by Colonel Edward Burleson in the army of General Houston. This company participated in the battle of San Jacinto, 21 April 1836, in which engagement Lemuel Blakely, of this company was killed and four others wounded, Billingsley himself was wounded in the left hand which rendered this hand crippled for life. In an article by J.K. Kuykendall, Tex. Hist. Association Quarterly, Vol. 4, April 1901, he states: "I arrived at Gonzales on the morning of March 6, 1836 and found there two companies to wit: Captain Jesse Billingsley's from Bastrop, and Captain Sherman's from Kentucky."

In "Coronado's Children," a book of tales of lost mines and buried treasures in the Southwest, by J. Frank Dobie (Southwest Press) Billingsley is credited with coining the famous phrase "Remember the Alamo! Remember Goliad!" which was used by the Texas troops as the battle cry as they charged the much larger Mexican army at the Battle of San Jacinto, April 21, 1836. The charge resulted in a complete victory and in the route of the Mexican Army.

This book says that such was the prowess of Captain Jesse Billingsley that his men were always proud to be known as the "Billingsley men." In a foot note this book says that during the battle General Houston sent word to Billingsley suggesting that he hold back his men from pressing the enemy; that Captain Jesse sent word back to the General about as follows: "Present my compliments to General Houston and tell him to go to H———."

Among his papers there are numerous letters showing the controversy between General Houston and himself regarding the conduct of the war for Independence.

(Comment———When this write up was received we suggested that the author of the book be consulted for a statement as to the authority for his statement therein about coining of the phrase. In a communication from him in 1932 he stated his authority for the statement emanated mostly from A.W. Billingsley. A communication from Mr. Billingsley states: "my information in regard to the cry is direct from the men that heard it; old man Andrews died at Rockport, had three boys, Jim, Dick and Tom; old man Sparks died 91 years old at Rockprot; Mr. Zuber, of Austin; Darlington and Scott, of Taylor, Texas; and Bill Harden of Angelina Co."He also states: "Lee Litton has a letter by Tom Andrews son of Mr. Andrews of Rockport whom I knew very well; I loaned her this letter now she says she lost it; it is very interesting and gives an account of uncle Jesse and how he cussed Houston at San Jacinto battlefield." The numerous letters regarding the conduct of the war, which we have seen, show his character clearly and the message he is said to have sent to General Houston is very characteristic of the man.)

Jesse Billingsley was born in Warren County, Tennessee 10 October 1810, moved to Missouri with his parents in 1817 and returned to Gibson County, Tennessee with them in 1827–1828, at age 43: immigrated to Texas in 1835.

He was a staunch and sturdy patriot and had a worthy part in the establishment of the great State of Texas, and served under three flags there, the Mexican, the Texas Republic, and the Stars and Stripes of the United States.

Later a report from Houston was: two of his men were killed, twenty three wounded, but the loss for the Mexican soldiers was six hundred and thirty killed plus they had taken Santa Ana prisoner. That victory brought a time of peace and the founding of the Republic of Texas and the people called themselves "Texians". They flew a flag for The Republic of Texas and it now waves proudly over the Alamo, a symbol of Texas freedom. The first president of the new Republic was Sam Houston and second was Mirabeau Buonaparte Lamar.

During the next few years the Mexican Government was still trying to cause trouble for the Texans and some of the Texas Citizens had become angered by the occasional invasions by Mexico. During this time it was a hard place to live with a lot of hard work. It was such a hard place that few women came here. The ones that did were of great mental strength, reliable, and had the ability to make do with very little.

The U.S. recognized Texas as Independent on March 3, 1837. It was Governor Lamar that approved the "Lone Star" flag to fly for their country in January of 1839, and he also proposed the town of Austin as the capital of Texas. The Lone Star flag is now the State flag of Texas.

In 1841 news was that Santa Ana had returned to power in Mexico which further angered the Texans, so late in 1842, Houston, who had been elected president for another term, sent a militia of volunteers on a raid into Mexico, but only half heartedly. It broke up along the way, and most members returned home. But around three hundred went on and elected their own commander. They became known as the "Mier Expedition". They attacked the town of Mier but ended up having to surrender, one hundred and seventy six men became prisoners on the evening of March 25, 1843.

Santa Ana ordered every tenth Texan would be executed. Originally Santa Ana wanted them all killed but the Governor of the State where they were held, refused that order. It was decided who was to die by putting seventeen black beans and one hundred fifty nine white beans in a clay jar, and shaken up, then each prisoner would take a bean. Black was death and white was life. On September 16, 1844 the ones that lived were released by Santa Ana. This is also referred to as the "Black Bean War".

Annexation of Texas came by authority of U.S. Congress and the president on December 29, 1845 but the final transfer from republic to statehood was on February 19, 1846.

Things were still not good between Mexico and Texas, so U.S. Army troops commanded by General Zachary Taylor was preparing to march from Corpus Christi to the Mexican border. Those troops had Been given orders by, the U.S. president, James K. Polk.

Mexico had still never admitted that Texas was an independent country, and there were still some threatening attacks on the Texans. General Taylor, and three thousand and nine hundred army soldiers made camp at Corpus Christi Bay near the Nueces River, as that had been the boundary since the days that Spain claimed all the area. Mexico was still claiming all the land between the Nueces and Rio Grande rivers.

Only the old Republic and later the U.S. considered the Rio Grande as the border between them.

Orders from President Polk reached Taylor telling him to take his army to the Rio Grande. Taylor knew by doing this it would look like a declaration of war toward Mexico but he was a General and so he obeyed the command.

On Sunday morning at ten o'clock, on March 8, 1846 Taylor and his soldiers started to march toward the Rio Grande. Mounted soldiers, called dragoons, three hundred seventy eight strong, were the first out. Then they were followed by supply wagons and horsedrawn guns. They marched through rain and mud, fought rattlesnakes and the sun and wind that dried out and cracked their lips and made their noses sore. The rest of the forces began leaving Corpus Christi Bay, for Mexico, the morning of March 9. They left in three large groups, called "brigades", March 9, 10 and 11. The men also traveled through dust and ankledeep sand that burned like hot coals. Late on March 28, 1846 the army neared their goal. As they looked across the River they could see the town of Matamoros. The soldiers were ordered to dig in here, and they built 'Fort Texas' out of dirt walls. Later the name was changed to Fort Brown and eventually became Brownsville. After a few weeks, they were attacked, and when word reached Polk he declared war against Mexico.

A man by the name of James Pinckney Henderson had recently been elected the first Governor of Texas and he left his office in charge of Lieutenant Governor Albert C. Horton, and set out as a major general, commanding an army of Texas and other volunteers, to fight against Mexico. There were more than eight thousand men serving with the U.S. forces. Texas Rangers were among the volunteers.

From information found in the trunk of one of Joel Curtis's daughters, he was listed on a registry of volunteers that signed up to fight during this last siege of the Mexican war. The sign up date was June 30, 1846 and on July 12, 1846 Joel was with the Arkansas Mounted Riflemen (volunteers) with Major Archibold Yell's 1st Regiment, Company H, under W.G. Preston's command, and Joel was listed as a private. They were headed for Texas and arrived at Camp Crockett near San Antonio, Texas on August 28, 1846.

I think about my greatgrandfather being there, fighting for the independence of Texas and the territories that were then our United States and am humbled by his willingness to fight for what he thought was right and it makes me very proud to be a Curtis.

Joel was put under Major Salon Borland and Captain C.C. Donley along with some 80 other soldiers. They were captured by the Mexican soldiers at Incarnation, Mexico and were held captive in Mexico City until August of 1848. According to documents from the archives of wars and military, Joel was absent from roll call on February 28, 1847, due to incarceration by the Mexican Government.

Major Yell's company, that had been the company Joel left Arkansas with, left San Antonio on August 31, 1847 headed for Buena Vista, Texas when they encountered the Mexican army, and Major Archibald Yell was reported to be the first that fell in the battle. Those that were left of his company then joined with General LasGaylon at Buena Vista and crossed the Rio Grande headed to Marmelou, Mexico on October, 31, 1847.

On December 31, 1847, the company arrived at Patos, Mexico, and continuing on came to Aqua Nerra, Mexico on February 28, 1848 after the loss of many brave men, including: Bowie, Crockett, Travis, and many, many others that were fighting for what they belived to be right.

On September 14, 1847, U.S. Forces under General Winfield Scott took control of Mexico City.

The battle was finally won, and a peace treaty was signed in February of 1848. This last battle fought gained the U.S. a vast region that included New Mexico, Arizona, California, Nevada, and Utah, also large parts of Wyoming and Colorado. Mexico finally gave up their claim to Texas and agreed to set the boundary at the Rio Grande. In return, the U.S. paid Mexico fifteen million dollars.

Joel was released from incarceration on August 2, 1848, at the close of the war, and was discharged on September 30, 1848 at New Orleans, Louisiana. It was reported that Major Salon Borland delivered to him, for services in the Mexican War, a land warrant of one hurdred and sixty acres, due to the Military Bounty Land Act of February 7, 1847.

There is a document from the U.S. government and signed by a deputy Clerk, Charles E. Thomas as being filed for on record the fifth day of April 1918 at 3:00 P.M. A homestead certificate number 1056, application 2546 which reads:*South half of the northwest quarter and the west half of the southwest quarter of section three in township seventeen south of Range Fourteen east of New Mexico Meridian in New Mexico Territory containing one hundred and sixty acres.*

A New Start

After his discharge Joel returned to Arkansas. Why? Did he have a reason, like a beautiful young woman, that he had met when he met the Dawsons in Kentucky? Did he have some relatives there that he did not speak of? What ever it was, we may never know, but return he did, and after his return he married Henrietta Cathrine Dawson in December of 1848. How he met her is still a mystery that may never be known, but he did meet and marry her, and at least we have knowledge from there.

One family researcher, Jody Weldy, speculates that Joel went to Arkansas because he may have had a sister and her husband living in Arkansas. We know that he was in Arkansas when he signed up for the Mexican War.

In the genealogy of Ethan and Elizabeth there was a daughter, Elizabeth. In the research there was found a Mary Elizabeth Curtis that married a Sabert Scott. These people showed up in Washington County Census, also in Crawford, and then Franklin County, which were cut out of Washington County. Joel was in these same places at the same time, so could they have been sister and brother–in–law?

Maybe some day it will come to light. The reason for this search was from a letter written by Joel and Rosa's oldest daughter, Hardin.

The letter was in Naomi's trunk and it stated "My half sister LuAnn Hanna has had a baby and she named him Joel after our father Joel Curtis", she added "The baby does not have Joel Curtis's coloring, he looks more like Aunt Lizzie Scott".

That caused the internet search for a Lizzie Scott and this Mary Elizabeth was found.

It seems they moved from Arkansas just a little before the Curtis, Dawson and related families did. They were somewhere close to where Joel, John, and the others moved to when they left Arkansas because Sabert was reported to be a member of Sloans Texas Rangers during Joel and John's stint in the service of the Texas Rangers. There was also evidence of ties from the Mexican War era. Joel being in H company under Captain Preston's command. The next higher up in the chain of command was Major Salon Borland that Joel was with when captured.

When tracing the history of the civil war era, Solan Borland commanded a regiment of Texas men that returned to Arkansas to fight for the confederated regular army, and apparently Sabert was one of the men that was sent with Borland's group. It was known that Borland was also from Franklin County, Arkansas.

The question still remains "What brought Joel to Arkansas, and when?" The thoughts of the researcher was, "It is doubtful Joel would have traveled one thousand and fifty two miles from Ohio to Arkansas, just to join the army, he could have joined in an Ohio regiment closer to home. After his discharge he did go back to Arkansas . He was a single young man that could have ventured anywhere he wanted, but didn't. "Did he go back because he had family there or had he already met Henrietta?"

There was another Scott family in the picture here also, Elizabeth 'DeGraftenried' married Andrew Kingery and had six children. Elizabeth was the middle child between Catherine and Luann DeGraftenried. The last child born to Elizabeth and Andrew was Mildred Kingery and she was born on March 4, 1849 in Franklin county, Arkansas where the family had moved sometime in 1848. That puts them in Arkansas with the rest of the DeGraftenried's, Dawson's, Curtis's, Miller's etc. . Andrew died in Arkansas, and some time later Elizabeth married a man named Scott, but his first name is unknown at this time. She and her new husband moved, along with all the other kin, so she ended up in Colfax County, New Mexico with the extended family, because the two younger daughters are in photos with the other family members.

So it stands to reason that this is the Aunt Lizzie that was mentioned in Aunt Hardin's letter to Aunt Naomi, because there is no proof anywhere that Sabert and Elizabeth Scott were in Colfax County, New Mexico, only in the Texas Census.

Henrietta Cathrine Dawson was the daughter of Thomas Henry and Letitia Louann DeGraftenried, Letitia was called 'Luzan' by her family. They had two children, John Barkley Dawson, born November 10, 1830 and Henrietta, born December 1832. They had traveled west, as far as Spring River, Missouri, Jasper County, from Hopkinsville, Trigg county, Kentucky, when John was 3 years old.

John and Henrietta had cousins, some Miller's, some DeGraftnrieds, and some other Dawson's that followed Thomas and Luzan's family as they slowly moved toward the west. According to John's recollections at one time, "They had lived at Spring River about six years." If this was right, from his memory, then Henrietta would have been seven years old when they left Missouri and headed further west.

Thomas found excellent farming country, around 1840, in Arkansas. He received a patent on land at Middle Township, Franklin County, Arkansas on December 1, 1849. They settled close to Fort Smith near the Arkansas river and Joel, thirty years old, married Henrietta, sixteen years old, in Franklin County, so I'm assuming that they were married at Thomas and Luzan's home.

The Dawson family and other kin' lived in Franklin County approximately ten years and after their marriage, Joel and Henrietta made their home near the Dawson's and through the years these family's were together. Joel still lived near the extended family for a time after her death.

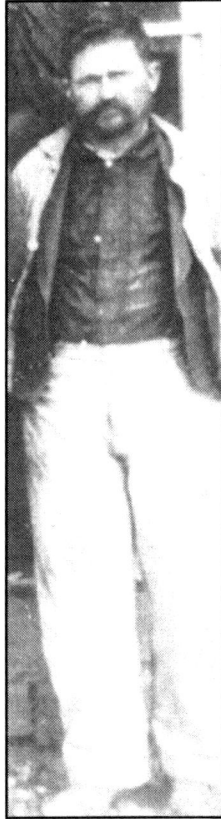

Richard 'Dick' Dawson Augustus Curtis
First son of Joel W. and Henrietta 'Dawson' Curtis

A year after their marriage, in December of 1849, a son was born, and they named him Richard Dawson Augustus. He was born in Crawford County, Arkansas and was known as 'Dick' Curtis. In a book written by Margaret Ward (granddaughter of Zenus Curtis) 'Cousins by the Dozens', "Dick was a mountain man, and was a scout for the Army. He and his brothers were good hunters and real marksmen with their guns. He knew the land around Taos, New Mexico but had died before her time and information about him was scarce". Zenas, Dick's younger brother said "It was Dick Curtis who helped cut the tall timbers from Red Lakes, New Mexico and hauled them to a place near the town of Dawson where he and his other brother's, Tom and Frank, built a comfortable home which was later destroyed by fire".

At the age of one year and ten months, in October 1851, Dick's little brother was born in Arkansas. They named him Joseph Thomas Henry and was called 'Tom'. In the same book by Margaret Ward she wrote "Tom was 'eccentric to say the least'. He never married, but spent his time hunting and fishing." Many tales were told about him but one that was really memorable. "Tom had a banty hen and was traveling from Texas to New Mexico when the hen decided to set. Tom hobbled his old white mule, 'Miss Katie', and patiently camped near the river until the chicks were hatched".

Naomi, Tom's younger half sister, had a letter from Tom in her trunk, with all the treasures she had kept, and he was telling her news of the family and his travels. 'Westward Ho' was not only Joel's words, but for many folks in the eastern and Mid American Territory's. We have heard this time and time again in our historic tales, from books to movies and school history.

We may see movies and read story's, but can we really put a sense to what it must have been like for these people. The hardships they encountered on these long treks across our vast country. The search was ever on for new and better places to settle for a more productive life.

In 1853 an influx of wagon trains headed west to California due to news reports of gold and fertile land. Some of the travelers camped along the Arkansas River to prepare for a long journey across vast plains and over high, and treacherous mountains.

The mountains being the Continental Divide. John Dawson, now a twenty three year old, young man, that apparently had absorbed lessons

12

in business from his father, may have questioned and listened to the people in the wagon train camps, and found out all he could about what it would take to make such a journey.

Joel must have been right in the middle of this, for all the Kin', and others with them decided to make preparations of their own for this move. The men must have had some excitement from what they had heard and maybe full of wonderful dreams about going to this new place, California, that every one was making out to be the end of the rainbow, and maybe a pot of gold for them there.

The route is not known for sure, but there is some evidence to indicate they traveled up the Arkansas River to the present site of Pueblo, Colorado, then on to where Denver is now located, with teams of oxen pulling their wagons. They decided, no doubt, that oxen would be tougher and easier to pull the wagons than a team of horses. About thirty years later at John's recollection "they crossed the Platte River (where Denver now stands) in 1853 and again in 1855 on their return trip". There was only a trail then, called the 'Emigrant Trail' to Salt Lake, Utah, and on to California".

There is no way of knowing for sure why the families left good land and homes in Arkansas to make a trek like this to a place that was known for it's lawlessness. An encampment known as Rough and Ready. It was an obscure gold mining town in Grass Valley not far from Dutch Flat in Nevada County (one of northern California's mountain counties, crossing the Sierras from the central valley to the Nevada Line). It's possible they may have been caught up in the talk of gold, striking it rich or some such hype, as this was the years of the great gold rush in California. It is also thought that they may have been with the Stockton Wagon Train, because Tom Stockton eventually became John's brother–in–law and best friend for life.

The families arrived at the encampment in September of 1853. Henrietta was expecting another child while on this trek and had the two young boys, Dick, not quite four years old and Tom, not yet two.

People now days complain while traveling in air conditioned and heated cars with rest stops, motels, and gas stations all along the nice paved roads. The children complain because their bored, "how much farther is it?" Do you think that all of us spoiled folk could handle a trip like they had? Just think about Henrietta, twenty one years old, with two small boys and six months pregnant. All that can be said from my point of view, "these people were tough and tenacious, with goals that they intended on reaching, no matter what".

Three months after arriving at Rough and Ready, Francis M. (the M. is thought to be Marion) Curtis, was born and they called him 'Frank'.

He was born in December of 1853, in Nevada County, California.

Rough and Ready seceded from the union in 1853, seven years before the state of South Carolina seceded. The small towns defiance attracted quite a few low lives and unsavory characters, most of which were new citizens that had left the old countries to save themselves from "who knows what".

At that time there were questions of 'slave' or 'free' states. This was probably utmost in the minds of the southerners. This place may have held a hope for the elusive 'freedom of choice', which also could have had something to do with their move to this place.

The family's were only there about two years and returned to Arkansas in 1855 going back the same route they took going up. Here again is Henrietta traveling in a wagon that is being pulled by a team of oxen with three young boys. Dick would now be six, Tom four and Frank two. I'm sure that the other women relations helped her with the boys as they made their trek back to Arkansas, but a trip like that had to have been hard, 'to say the least'. It would be interesting to know what their life was like while in such a rough place and what Joel, John, Thomas and the other men did to provide for their families.

On May 3, 1854 a news account, in the Van Buren 'Arkansas intelligencer', spoke of cattle drives from Arkansas to California. John may have seen this or heard talk of it and having a good business mind probably discussed this with Joel and the other relatives of buying a herd of cattle and trailing them to California. They must have figured that the mining camps would pay good money for good beef on the hoof. Living there for two years made it possible for them to know what the demand would be.

This started a lot of years on the dusty trails for these two brother'sinlaw along with many others, some being John's cousins and a few other men were hired along the way. One of the men that was hired was Clay Allison and some of the kin' were Miller's, Stockton's, and DeGraftenried's.

This generation of folk, living in this era, were always living on the edge, and most of them were known during the pages of famous cattlemen, frontiersmen, trail blazers, cowboys, drovers, soldiers, scouts, Indian fighters and some were even called fortune hunters or adventurists.

So many times it was said "well, so and so sure left home at an early age." Unfortunately, for the Curtis family that is probably why we have a lot of blank years for Joel. He must have ventured from home as a very young man or 'boy', but it was our blessing and fortune when he married Henrietta and joined himself to the Dawson family, because through them we do have some legacy of his life, and also because of our wonderful Naomi that kept every note,every letter, every piece of paper and document for preservation for her descendents.

It seems that John Dawson, on the other hand, was an exception to the rule where his family was concerned. He always wanted his family close no matter where he went or what he decided to do and because of this, Joel had someone that cared a lot for him and we now have a part of Joel to remember down through all generations. I'm judging that only by hard work and loving companionship and dependency on each other did these families live and survive through all the hardships and deaths they encountered.

In John's autobiography of 1885, the enterprising idea for a cattle drive to California, he states "I returned to California in the fall of 1855. I drove a herd of cattle from Arkansas to California and located at the Butte Mountains near Marysville." John did not think of himself as a cowboy but instead a 'drover'. His 'drovers' that were with him on this drive were Joel Curtis (brother–in–law), Tom Stockton (future brother–in–law), Jasper DeGraftenried and Tom Miller (cousins) and the Lacy's that were old friends.

These same men all trailed herds many, many times together and just some of the hardships that they underwent were, rain and thunderstorms that some times caused cattle stampede's, rattle snakes, dust storms, heat and cold, cattle rustlers and Indian attacks. They were unable to carry a lot of provisions with them and what they did take had to be something that wouldn't ruin like hard tac or jerky. When pushing a large herd of cattle along with a string of horses some of the men had to ride behind, and to the side of the herd to control it, and while doing so became covered with the dirt from the trails during long stretch's between water.

In records and accounts that John recalled, he recommended three Littrell brothers, Marion, Lige and George that were all good cowhands, that he had hired at one time or other. John also remembered Clay Allison as a hot tempered, unstable, hairtrigger fingered young man that drank a lot but was a 'top hand'. Clay's life was intertwined with the Dawson's, Curtis's, Miller's, DeGraftenried's, Chase's, and the other neighbors after moving to New Mexico. Clay was reported to be the nearest neighbor, to the Chases, that lived on the Poñil. He was talked about in the town of Cimarron as having a loose tongue, and tales about his wild sprees, while drinking, manytimes ending in some wild shooting, and riding his horse into some stores. It seemed, although he was a reckless, wild and crazy guy,the women all liked him. He loved it where there was music and dancing, and was a gentleman while at parties. He attended most of the party's and was said to be a very handsome man with a charming way toward all the ladies.

From all the cattle drives the men learned where the best trails were and the first drive was probably the same route the family's had traveled twice before. The Emigrant Trail wasn't yet an established thoroughfare, but it did have a few advantages. They knew where there was water, and the places were scouted for rest and grazing of the herds. There were Forts where they could get supplies or help if necessary. This trail was more northern than the Sante Fe Trail and actively used from 1824 to 1844.

From 1855 to 1861 Joel, John and John's relatives, friends, and hired hands 'drove' cattle together.

During the time between 1853 and 1857 they encountered Kit Carson and had a long talk with him. According to Margaret Ward, in her book, she states that "Dick Curtis was a good friend of Kit Carson." At one time, Kit during his lifetime, had lived on the Poñil where the Chase's bought and lived. Kit told John, at this chance meeting, of some open country, in Young County, Texas, that was a newly established Fort, called Fort Belknap.

In the Spring of 1857, Joel, John and the extended families plus other kin', moved to Young County, Texas. Another reason for the move to this area was because of the allotment of land for homesteads. They were more generous settlements than in other U.S. territories. Texas offered six hundred and forty acres (a mile square section) for Thomas Dawson as head of household and another three hundred and twenty acres to

John, who was still a single man. Combined right to homestead was one thousand acres for the Dawson family. The other kin helped settle on this land and were there 10 years from 1857 to 1868. I know that Joel and Henrietta were there, but no mention of them in the information I have to go on as to whether they received land, but we know that they were in the vicinity as to census reports and reports where other of their children were born.

John started buying and selling cattle as a business. The land they chose had a lot of advantages for raising cattle. John's family, and friends worked the cattle for and with him, and in my own mind Joel must have started getting some cattle together of his own for there is evidence that he drove and sold cattle of his own during the drives to Colorado.

John and his drovers, started driving some of these cattle shortly after he accumulated enough to make it worth while. The route they were taking was pioneered and blazed by John, and from 1859 through 1860 it became known as the Dawson Trail, which went northeast out of Fort Belknap to the Arkansas River then followed the river to Pueblo, Colorado, and north to Denver. They took this trail on all their drives in 1860, and for a time, until 1866 when they decided to take a different route.

They went from Fort Belknap west to Fort Sumner, New Mexico, north to Fort Union and into Pueblo.

Charles Goodnight also had blazed a trail up into Colorado from the area of Fort Belknap. His father's name was Charles, and was born in 1806 in Kentucky. Charles Senior grew up in Kentucky and married Charlotte Collier. In 1828 they moved to southern Illinois. Because of malaria that was common in that country the family moved again to Prairie County near Madison. On March 5, 1836, three days after the declaration of Texas independence, Charles Jr. was born. In 1841 Charles Sr. died of pneumonia, and Charlotte then married a farmer named Hiram Daugherty. In late 1845 the family moved to Texas. They rented a farm near the Brazos, and close to where the Dawson and Curtis families eventually moved.

Shortly after settling here, Charlotte left Hiram and again was a woman in a hard country with a family to feed. Charles Jr. had three siblings, two older and one younger and three months after leaving Hiram, she had a baby.

In 1848 they moved to Port Sullivan. Charles and his brother both hired out to jobs starting at the ages of fifteen and eleven. In 1853, his mother married a preacher by the name of Adam Sheek and in 1856 Charles and his stepbrother, J. Wes Sheek, that was three years younger, formed a partnership.

The two boys then contracted to take a herd of cattle, four hundred and thirty head, and keep them on shares for ten years. Thus Charles Goodnight was in the cattle business at a time of learning and building on his knowledge of ranching. They settled on a place on the Brazos a year before John Dawson and Joel Curtis moved there.

In 1857 as the Curtis and Dawson clans moved there, Goodnight and Sheek trailed up the Brazos into Palo Pinto County, and made permanent camp at Black Springs in the Keechi Valley. Soon after their move to the Keechi they met Oliver Loving.

Charles thought Loving was the most experienced cowman on the northwest fringe and had some influence on Goodnight's life.

Mr. Loving ran a small country store that was located on the Belknap Road. He also owned a few slaves and a good sized herd of cattle. Most of the cattle that were grown here were marketed through him. He usually trailed them, because of distance, hardship, and dangers, to Shreveport, Alexandria or New Orleans. In 1858 along with John Durkee, he decided to take a herd north. It was a long, hard and weary drive. They had to cross a dozen streams and ended up in the markets in Illinois.

During that year the 'Colorado Gold Rush' began. They heard that Denver County was being flooded by people that would make an awesome beef market. These became Goodnight, Loving, Dawson and Curtis Markets, being John and Joel's first markets in Colorado. They knew as before in the California mining camps that these mining towns in Colorado would also be great.

On August 29, 1860 Mr. Loving had a thousand steers headed for the mining camps in Colorado, and John hired on as his guide. There is no information that proves Joel was with John, and may not have been, but most of the time he was with John, especially on John's drives, so it is possible that he may have been with him here also.

Goodnight helped the Loving herd get past 'The Cross Timbers' and waited until they crossed the Red River and seen them head a course into the Indian Nation. ('*The Cross Timbers*,' *was a very unique natural hedge, consisting mostly of hardwoods such as post oak, blackjackoak and elm, and separated by prairie into eastern and western wedges, stated by an observer in the mid1800's).*

The men came to the Arkansas River just below the Great Bend and followed it into Pueblo and on north. They wintered the herd on grass country where Goodnight eventually established a ranch. When the snow melted, the next spring, Loving pushed into Denver and sold out to the miners and prospectors.

In the mean time, in the early months of 1858, back in Texas the Indian raids had increased dramatically and the people were trying to get the reserves of tribes moved out of the Territory. One reason for this was the murders of the Mason, and Cameron families.

Sometime about the 24th of April 1858 an Indian raid in the area of Fort Belknap resulted in all horses there becoming the stolen property of the raiders.

Charles Goodnight's neighbor Isaac Lynn decided he should make a visit to his daughter and son–in–law's place about twenty miles from his ranch in a place called Lost Valley, in Jack County. He was about sixty years of age and walked everywhere he went. He raised and sold good horses, but never rode.

He took his rifle and when he got to Thomas Mason and his daughter's place he found her in the cow coral. She had been shot and had her baby in her arms.

He said "The baby had been nursing its dead mother and was still alive." They had another child about two or three and it was still in the house alive.

Mr. and Mrs. James Cameron lived in the same cabin, it was like our modern day duplexes, with two separate living quarters in the same building. These houses were called dog–trot–double–pen cabins, or just double–pen cabins. The double–pen cabin was where the building was all one and had two door entrances, one to each side in the front of it. The dogtrot style was two cabins together with a breezeway between them with the doors each facing the breezeway (an open space averaging ten feet in width) with a common roof covering the two pens and the breezeway.

The Camerons also had a child, a boy about ten years old and they had also been killed, but the Indians had taken the boy. Mr. Lynn took his two grandchildren to Jacksboro and told of the murders and stolen horses.

The Indians had roped a wild mule and tied the Cameron boy on it. The mule was driven along with the stolen horses. An emigrant train was passing on their way to California along the Mercer – California Trail when the Indians came in sight of them headed northwest. The Horsemen took after them but they could not catch them.

As they started back to the wagons they rode through some tall grass where the little boy was, and he yelled as he jumped up, "I'm here yet!"

According to the boy's story they took him off the mule and put him on a horse with a redhaired man that spoke English. When they saw the wagon train men coming after them, the man shoved the boy off and told him "Stay here until I come back."

The boy was really tired so he lay down and fell asleep. When he heard the riders he thought it was the redheaded man coming back for him. He told them who he was and what had happened, and they sent him with an escort to Belknap and back to Mr. Lynn.

Buck Berry and Tom Stockton were given commissions to raise Companies of frontiersmen, and according to 'The White Man' newspaper "There are no, two, better Rangers on the Frontier."

Colonel Jack Baylor was in command of two hundred and fifty men that left out in January 1861, and under pretences of being 'buffalo hunters', were in high spirits, in search of the Goodnight Trail but they were actually searching for the ones that had murdered the Masons and Camerons. After a hundred miles of nothing but dry and desolate land, they came into Wichita hungry, and half afoot, in poor shape with no luck of their search. Tom Stockton had been scout and guide on this excursion.

Of all accounts the murderers were never caught or brought to justice, and the country was still ill at ease, for the most part, but life went on.

The years that John and Joel were trailing cattle into Colorado there were also historically known men that were following the Goodnight Trail, men like John Chisum, Tom Boggs and Frank Pope.

After the Civil War broke out, John started raising cattle for the cavalry troops at Fort Sumner, NM, Fort Union, Fort Marcy, Fort Bascom, and Fort Belknap that also distributed beef to the Indians.

(Samuel) Zenus Albert Curtis (born to Joel W. and Henrietta 'Dawson' Curtis)

Mary Francis 'Todhunter' Curtis

    In December of 1857, on the eighth day of the Month, Henrietta had another son. Zenus Samuel Albert Curtis was born in Parker County, Texas. Some time later they moved closer to Fort Belknap, Young County and settled on the Brazos River, in Miller Valley.

    A story told about Zenus, "when he was a boy, the Curtis boys did not attend school much, but one day Zenas and several boys his age were walking along scuffing their feet in the dirt, when they saw a group of girls going toward the small school which was hidden in the nearby foothills. Someone suggested they catch up with the girls and the chase was on. One of the girls was Mary Todhunter and she told the group to hide in the cheekcherry bushes and let the boys go by. The ruse worked, and the boys arrived breathless and spent, to find no girls in sight. Of course, the girls eventually appeared, and this was the first time Zenas got a glimpse of his future wife."

Because of the Civil War, Charles Goodnight joined the troopers in Texas as a scout. Being a scout and plainsman fit Charles well, as above all, scouts had to have an instinct, or sense for direction without having to depend on a compass. Charles was a plainsman and had wandered this country in darkness and storms and was always able to keep his destination in his mind and got there no matter what things came upon him. Not only was he a scout and guide, he was also a regular Ranger. Charles was in the Rangers under Captain Jack Cureton, and between 1858 and 1861 he stated, "The extreme western settler, in Young County, at the outbreak of the war, lived four miles west of Belknap, and there was nothing west from there to the Rocky Mountains."

On January 22, 1858 Buchanan County was formed out of Young County and on February 1, 1858 Joel is on a list of signers trying to get Major Neighbors removed from being in charge of the Indian reservation *(also called the reserves)*, for not handling his office appropriately.

According to J. Evetts Haley's book on Charles Goodnight, with a statement about Neighbors "He was hopeful and energetic, worked with conscience and zeal to make the reserves a success. A suspicion of raiding attached to the reserve Indians, but Neighbors denied the truth of the reports. Late in 1857 there was much complaint from the border people, and petitions were addressed to the Secretary of the Interior asking for the removal of Neighbors, who replied "The thievery was the work of wild Indians and renegade whites, magnified and capitalized by his enemies, and should be discounted in whole". And he had enemies, chief among whom was John R. Baylor, who made capital of every raid. Baylor, then part and parcel of the frontier, was appointed agent at the Comanche Reserve in 1856, where he served until dismissed in May, 1857."

In late 1859 cattle were purchased by John to sell at Pikes Peak. The cattle that were purchased were trailed by the way of the Dawson Trail to Colorado and sold to Colonel Francisco Chavez.

This same year a slave of 'Joe' Curtis named Jno, was killed by Indians. He was returning from Picketville, and was mortally wounded by several Indians, at a point a few miles north of the present city of Breckenridge. Jno's leg was amputated, but this did not save him, for he died in a short time. 'Joe' Curtis then lived in Miller's Valley, on the Clear Fork. 'The author personally interviewed Jno. Irwin, James Clark, and others who were living in Stephens County, and adjoining counties at the time." The Indians were still raiding and killing folks all in the area and Rangers were sent out all the time to track them down and some were caught but a lot of them were able to elude the trackers.

Joel was enumerated in the 1860 slave schedule census in Buchanan County and three mulatto slaves were listed in his household. In the November 3, 1850 slave schedule Joel was enumerated and also in the October 28, 1850 census Joel, Henrietta and Dick were enumerated. By all these accounts we know that Joel had slaves while living in Texas and elsewhere during a period of 1850 through 1860's. I'm sure they were there with Henrietta and the children during the years that Joel was off trailing herds of cattle to California, New Mexico and Colorado and probably were a great help to her and Joel, not leaving her totally alone during these bad times of Indian raids and uprisings. Her extended family was there but all the young hands and men were either off fighting in the war or off chasing the Indians, which most times left the women and children without men to protect them, so having slaves was a real plus.

According to a September 15, 1860 article in the Weatherford, Parker County, Texas newspaper called the 'White Man' a notice was written to 'The People' of Buchanan County, August 2, 1860. This notice was undersigned by G.W. Hagler, Joseph V. Howell, *J.W. Curtis*, Wm. R. Hill, John Snyder, *Gaddis E. Miller Sr., Gaddis E.Miller Jr., John B. Dawson*, W. L. Browning, Wm. Hitson, Geo. Greer, and Jo. Matthews.

The statement of these signers was:

"A man named L.G. Collins, that they knew to be a 'brave', 'fearless' man and bold defender of the frontier, and that he was a bitter enemy to the Indians and their friends, was murdered at his residence on Clear Fork of the Brazos." The report claimed, "A party of citizens and Rangers had manufactured a false report that Mr. Collins was a notorious horse thief so they could commit the murder of this man for the large amount of money he had."

The men asked for proof of the claims, and asked why they had killed Collins before they had proof of the allegations. In this notice they demanded the arrest and trial of the men, and until they established Mr. Collin's guilt and their innocence, they should stand before the world as murderers and robbers, and they deserved the scorn and contempt of all just men.

There was no following report on the finality of this matter so it is left to one's own judgment as to the outcome.

In the fall of 1860 the group of drovers that were friends and family, used the Dawson Trail again but Mr. Loving was along on this drive, with another herd headed to Colorado. During this drive and with Joel away again, Henrietta had a daughter in October. The name given to her was Alvia S. Curtis. After four sons, Joel and Henrietta had a girl. What a joy for the family to a have a girl after having several boys.

While in Colorado Mr. Loving was arrested and put in jail for being a confederate and Joel, John and John's drovers returned to Texas by way of the Santa Fe Trail, and the Pecos River. Loving had also, at some time, become friends of Kit Carson, Lucien Maxwell, and some other prominent Mountain men and with their help he was let go. He left his outfit and took a stage coach to St. Joseph and reached home on August 9, 1861.

In May of 1861, Joel and Henrietta had another son, John Barkley Curtis, and they called him 'Johnny', or some called him 'Bark'. He was born at Palo Pinto, Buchanan County, which on December 17, 1861, was changed to Stephens County.

On September 1, 1861 John Dawson married Tom Stockton's twenty year old half sister, Edwena, in San Antonio, Texas. On December 15, 1862 Edwena had a son, Augustus Green Dawson and they called him 'Gus'.

Less than a year later on December 1, 1863 Edwena died. This was a terrible blow to John and now he was a widower with a baby son to raise. Thomas and Luzan took the boy and kept him with them while John was out on his drives.

In December of 1862 Joel enlisted in the Texas Rangers. John had also enlisted according to a statement he had made "My wife died December 21, 1863. I joined the Texas Rangers where we had to serve one fourth of our time. We were organized to protect the frontier of Texas. The service was exclusively for the state in watching and keeping the bands of wandering Indians and Mexicans out... I remained a member of the Rangers for four years." Again the brothers–in–law were riding together but for a different reason. Joel became Captain of Company 'M', Texas

Cavary (volunteers). He was also required to serve one fourth time which was four months of the year.

Sometime in 1863 a report of Joel's son, Thomas or Tom as they called him, was attacked by a panther, while at the Miller Creek School, in Stephans County. This was the total of information I had about this incident but he must not have been hurt too bad as he grew up to be a man.

In that same year Henrietta gave birth to Tscharner D. Curtis and they called him 'Charner' the 'Ts' being silent. He was also born at Palo Pinto, Stephens County, about the same time this year the Indians raided John Dawson's ranch trying to take his horses but were unsuccessful in their endeavors.

On December 15, 1863 an act was passed to provide extra protection to the frontier. TST (Texas State Troopers) was formed. This was at the time John Dawson joined, while these troopers were being formed.

This was during the civil war and sometimes the men that protected the frontier were also called Texas Militia or Texas Mounted. They were considered Texas Rangers because they performed a service of defending the frontier against Indians, not fighting with the Confederacy against Union Soldiers. There was a lot of confusion over all the names used by people of who or who wasn't a Texas Ranger because some Confederate units were called Texas Rangers, simply because, their members originated from Texas.

These groups were soldiers, not Texas Rangers.

The most well known of these, was Terry's Texas Rangers. The only ones that were real Texas Rangers were the ones who remained to fight the Indians while the others joined the war.

Information taken from the *TEXAS RANGER HALL OF FAME AND MUSEUM* in Waco, Texas under *"Texas Rangers in the Civil War Era"* on *Texas State Troopers (TST) 1861–1865 Frontier Regiment/ Frontier Organization* as follows:

"Perhaps one of the most confusing periods of Texas Ranger history is the Civil War Era. During the 1860's Texas was essentially in a war on two fronts. Throughout the civil war, the Texas State legislature provided laws and appropriations to organize companies of men to provide frontier defense. Early in the civil war, young men in Texas had the option of enlisting in local militia units for frontier protection, instead of going off to war. As the civil war continued on, more and more of these young men enlisted in the Confederacy and went off to fight against the Union. However, as these young men left their homes, many settlements on the Texas frontier were left vulnerable to Indian raids. Counties and settlements within the counties often continued to organize State Troopers to protect themselves. As the national conflict continued and more young Texans joined the Confederacy, the men left home to defend the Texas frontier were more often in their thirties and forties.

These Texas State Troopers were not part of the Confederate States Army but served under the command control of officers in the employ of the State of Texas, although the organization of the troops was along military lines. The first of these groups was the Frontier Regiment which existed from mid–1861 until December of 1863 when the group was mustered into the CSA. They were replaced by the Frontier Organization which may have been in existence until the end of the war in 1865. In the official State records these groups are often referred to as 'The Texas State Troopers.'"

A short description of the organization and responsibilities of these units can be found in the "New Handbook of Texas" vol. 3 see entries for 'Frontier Regiment and Frontier Organization.' A more indepth treatment of State Troopers during the years 1861–1865 can be found in David Paul Smith's 'Frontier Defense in The Civil War.'

In a segment of 'Frontier Defense' page 146 'A Sergeant A.D. Miller, in command of an eight man squad in Stephans County, states "They came upon a party of at least twenty Indians moving in a northwesterly direction. These Indians probably represented the main body of the party attacked earlier in Eastland County, by Gilbert's men. Miller followed the trail approximately fifteen miles, overtook the hostiles, and attacked. Captain J.W. Curtis, of Stephens County, later described the battle to Major Quayle, 'the fight lasted about an hour.'"

This account goes on to tell that by February of 1864, there were added problems. They now had trouble from deserters of the enlisted men of the Civil War. Most of the troubles came from a large number of renegades from the midst of the deserters.

During this time another problem arose from desertions reported from 'The Frontier Regiment', Erath, George B., surveyor, Texas Ranger and a Captain in the days of The Republic of Texas and a Major in the Frontier organization during the civil war from '*Texas State Library and Archives Commission*', reported that his district not only had a large number of Captain Lloy's men but also of Captain Whitesides company, all but one man and himself, deserted.

According to Charles Goodnight, 'As if things weren't bad enough' a terrible drought fell over the Country from 1863 through 1864. The Brazos River dried up and trees and crops withered and failed.

On January 6, 1864, three frontier districts were formed. The First Frontier District was commanded by Brigadier General J.W. Throckmorton, and second in command was Major Wm. Quayle.

Stephens County had two detachments, which were: number one, Captain Jack J. Cureton, (the same Cureton that Charles Goodnight rode with), with fifty six men: number two, *Captain* J.W. Curtis, with fifty seven men. There were a total of one hundred and thirty one enlisted troops for Stephens County.

December 30, 1864 General Throckmorton, at Dove Creek, gave a command for troops to follow an Indian Party. On or about January 6, 1865 Captain Curtis and Captain Dellahunty's troops turned back to home base in Stephans County. On January 8th the other commands attacked the Indians at Dove Creek, Tom Green County, Texas. Toward the end of January Captain Curtis reported to Major Quayle his feelings about punishing the troops that took part in the Dove Creek Battle. Sometime in March of 1865 Joel resigned from the Texas Rangers.

In the spring of 1866 cattle were gathered again. On August 17th of that same year, Goodnight, Loving, Dawson, and Curtis combined, drove their cattle toward Colorado and in late fall part of the herd was sold to General Carleton at Fort Sumner. They wintered the rest of the herd on the Pecos River near Fort Sumner.

In the spring of 1867 the remainder of the herd was driven to Colorado and sold to J.W. Iliff in Denver, and records show that on December 1, 1866 Mr. Iliff wrote a check to Joel Curtis for $886.40 for cattle purchased from him. After the whole herd had been sold they returned to Texas.

The summer of 1867, six thousand head of cattle were purchased and as before, Curtis, Chase, Dawson and Maulding were headed to Colorado with them.

Again they wintered the herd near Fort Sumner. The Spring of 1868 they arrived in Denver and again sold the herd to Mr. Iliff.

At this time John Dawson met with Goodnight and formed a partnership. Charles Goodnight, John Dawson and Joel Curtis, while returning to Texas, met some other herders on the Pecos River, purchased the herds, and returned to Colorado with them.

The fall of that same year Dawson and Goodnight ended their partnership. Somewhere along the way Joel Curtis and John Dawson went separate ways. I have no information to let me know where John had been but while returning home, met up with Joel and Taylor 'Tom' Maulding on their way to purchase land from Lucien B. Maxwell, on the Vermejo River, in northern New Mexico Territory. Curtis and Maulding described the land to John as being "Mountains, rivers, and creeks, wide valleys and thousands of acres of fine grazing land. That there were minerals, timbers, game in abundance such as deer, antelope and bear and the rivers were alive with fish." They told him they needed thirty seven hundred dollars, because they lacked that much cash, to conclude the purchase. I think they must have been trying to figure out how to raise that much money when John came along. John told them "I have enough money necessary for the purchase with me," so they told him if he would put that money into helping purchase the land he could have first pick.

The New Mexico Territory was a wild and undeveloped country with economic and political troubles after the civil war ended, as was so for much of the western country. It had become a United States Territory in 1846 following the occupation of American troops under the command of General Stephan Watts Kearny, and the organization of it as a Territory was in 1850 and in 1861 there was an invasion of Confederated troops.

After the Confederate troops left, going to Texas, Union troops from California came in with New Mexico Volunteers headed up by Colonel Kit Carson, and fought against the Navajo and Apache.

Before John purchased the land that Joel Curtis and Tom Maulding told him about, another young man and his wife purchased land from Mr. Maxwell. About two hundred acres of the land that was northeast along the foothills from Maxwell's place, past the Pŏnil, and past the mouths of two other large canyons, towards the Vermejo. That couple was Manley Chase and his wife Theresa.

Manley's father had come from Wisconsin, along the Sante Fe Trail, in 1857. The wagon train they were in was attacked by Comanche Indians and those that survived made their way back to Franklin, Missouri. When the Colorado gold rush began the following year his father came across, again on the Sante Fe Trail, to Central City, Colorado. He married a widow with a daughter four years younger than Manley.

Her name was Theresa, and they were married in 1860. The couple had two children that tragically died and so they decided to move to New Mexico Territory and start their lives over. That is when they met and bought land from Mr. Maxwell.

The next year on a July morning Maxwell introduced John Dawson, Joel Curtis, and Tom Stockton to Manley Chase. They had trailed another herd of cattle from Texas into Colorado, and came back after looking at the land the previous fall. They had a good visit, and reminisced about the cattle they had been driving all these years, the Civil War days, Indian uprisings, hard times, and some of the good ones. They discussed the Vermejo land and they all rode up to look at the land again.

On their way to look at the land they went by Manley's place and Theresa invited them to come back for dinner. They went on up to the land that Joel, Taylor or 'Tom' as they called him, and John had first talked about and had seen once before. On this day John chose his land first, according to the agreement made with Joel and Tom.

At this time John told Manley "Some of us are comin' out this fall, but most of our families won't be here till the spring. I plan on buyin' two or three hundred head out of this herd I'm bringing to Fort Sumner for the winter. We all aim to run our cattle together, form a pool, you might say. Want in on It?"

Manley told him he sure did and asked John to buy about a hundred head for him. This began a long friendship and also a business partnership.

After Joel and Tom received money from John to conclude the sale of the Maxwell land, Joel bought his property separately. His ranch was on "the Upper part", the Caliente drainage into the Vermejo, and Curtis Canyon. On the 7th day of January 1869, an indenture was made between Lucian B. Maxwell and Luz Maxwell nu Baubien of Mora County, Territory of New Mexico, to Joel W. Curtis of the same County, for seventeen hundred dollars, which is on record. It states that his land connects to Taylor Maulding and Richard D. Miller. Curtis Canyon is still named the same.

A story told by Zenus Curtis in his later years was that John and Joel, on a trip back to Texas for cattle to stock their ranches, bought twelve thousand head of cattle. On their way back while crossing the plains, the task became tremendous, as the raiding Indians in ever increasing numbers drove off the herds or killed the animals, until the very weary drivers finally reached their home range with only one hundred and forty three head.

The land that was purchased by John was the entire watershed of the Vermejo River, approximately thirty eight sections, some twenty four thousand acres. He paid six point five cents an acre for it. Joel took the piece of land near the mouth of the canyon.

As usual all the kinfolks were willing to follow John, Joel and Tom in their purchase of new land and a promise of a good life there. Joel, Tom, and Richard Miller all moved to the New Mexico land from Texas in the fall of 1868 and John went on a business trip to Denver but also had a second motive. That was to find a wife. He ended up at Veal's Station in Texas, as his search in the Denver area showed no promise. His mother, father, and son Gus met him upon his arrival in Texas. It was here that he met Laura Stout that had been a school teacher at Veal's Station. They were married on September 1, 1868 in Texas then traveled to their new land in New Mexico. The other kin' of John and Henrietta moved also.

They built homes and started a new life, planting fruit trees and starting up some good herds on the fertile, lush grasslands. The most northern part of the drainage called the Caliente, on the Vermejo River, became Joel's place. Manley Chase purchased more land here along with these men and he, Tom and Richard divided up the other parts. The Van Bremmers were west and the Caliente to the north and the Lacy's were to the south. In the same winter of 1868, Henrietta bore Joel another son and they named him Joel Warner after his father and grandfather.

There had been a small Spanish community, for sometime, at the location John chose to settle on. He and Laura moved into one of the adobe buildings which later became known as 'Poverty Row' by the family!

Since Manley and Theresa Chase lived nearby, Theresa and Laura became life long friends. While their husbands were away working, all the women and children of the tiny settlement had outings together such as berry picking for wild plums in season. They were most likely used for making pies and Jelly or Jam.

Laura bore John two children and about six weeks after the birth of their second child on June 2, 1872, Laura died. Siria Milton, called 'Si', was the first of the children born and Abner Bruce the last one.

This left John a widower again and with three children to raise on his own and was once again grieving at the loss of a wife. It was also a terrible blow for Theresa as she had come to love Laura as she would have a sister.

The boys again were placed with family but this time Laura's parents took her two boys. In a statement made by John later, he said that he had taken Gus with him "The boy being about nine or ten now," on a cattle drive.

Again John needed someone in his life to help him raise his three boys so he again went in search of a wife. Just by coincidence and a little finagling he met and married an 'old maid' school teacher by the name of Lavinia Jefferson from Middletown, Iowa on May 28, 1873.

The cattle business was flourishing. Through the years, Joel, John, Manley, Tom, and some others formed several associations to run cattle on the open prairies and the cattle were then trailed and sold to various markets, most of the time to army posts or forts.

Not long after moving here these families in this small community became well known and highly thought of throughout the territory and beyond.

Joel, at some point in time, had some cattle stolen by the Kiowa and Comanche tribes of Indians. According to a Journal of the House of Representatives of the U.S. Government, on February 1, 1869 a paper was filed by Joel for reimbursement for said property. The matter was then referred to the committee on Indian affairs. Joel's name also comes up along with seventy one others, on an appropriation, from a motion by Mr. Garfield, to pay for the stolen goods of these people. It was dated January 13, 1874. There was a T.D. Curtis among these names. No related information puts to mind that he was some of our kin but there is none that says he wasn't.

In Joel's obituary dated June 9, 1904 from the 'Cloudcroft Silver Lining', a newspaper from Cloudcroft, New Mexico, stated that "He received eleven thousand dollars from the government a few years ago for cattle stolen by the Indians."

While the men and women of this new place worked on their land, clearing brush and getting the land leveled as much as possible, they would often see Utes and Apaches coming down the canyon on their way to town to get their government rations.

I have read and heard stories that these settlers and others throughout New Mexico Territories would provide some home grown vegetables, milk, bread, home churned butter, and anything else they thought the Indians would take, and in turn the Indians would leave them alone as they roamed throughout the countryside,

The site that the Miller family chose was where the Vermejo left the Mountains. There was already a small shack here that had been used sometimes by people traveling a trail through this part of the country. They added on the little shack and made a contract with some freighters to operate a stage stop.

All spring of 1868, the valley was noisy with the building of homes, barns, corrals, and what ever else they needed for getting by. The women were working hard alongside their husbands trying to make homes from the houses that were being built, plus keeping them and the children fed, clothed, schooled, and protected from the hazards of that day and time.

There were bad times also such as the sad news this same year. John Dawson, while in Colorado, had heard news that he came home with. He said "Kit Carson had been taken to the hospital at Fort Lyons by Tom and had died on May 23rd at the age of fifty eight."

It was told to John that Kit had been sick, for a year or more, after a horse fell on him about two or three years back. He had been having bad pain in his chest ever since.

Carson resigned as commander of Fort Garland, Colorado in 1867, and had decided to buy land from St. Vrain on the Purgatory, so he could just take it easy, but it didn't come to pass.

During the spring of 1868 he went to Taos and moved his family to the Tom Bogg's place until his wife Josefa had her baby. They had six other children but this seventh one had caused complications for her and approximately two weeks after the baby was born, Josefa died. Kit had such a deep love for her and according to some of his close friends he quit eating and just sat outside the house with his chest hurting, from his fall, all this time.

There were many, many people that mourned the loss of this great frontiersman and friend. Manley stated that "Kit and Maxwell go back a long way as far as tales go," for Lucien Maxwell had related stories to Manley which he loved hearing and made the statement that "he never knew Kit personally but sure wished he had."

Lucien told of the time, in 1842, when Kit was a guide for Fremont. Maxwell was a hunter for that expedition. The trip was up to the Wind River in Wyoming Territory and down over the Sierras in the middle of winter. The story was, "Kit went over the mountains as if he'd done it many times before."

Kit and Josefa, had for a time, lived down at the Rayado, and used Tom Bogg's cabin on the Pónil, during the time in the 50's, when he was Indian Agent. He was going to be sorely missed by a lot of people.

In 1869, news from Cimarron was that Mora County had been divided and the new half had been named after Vice President Colfax. This is where Cimarron, and the Vermejo were and where Joel, John and the others all lived. It then became Colfax County, and Elizabeth Town was made the County seat. At this same time Lucian had been appointed judge.

Manley and Theresa purchased the Pónil land from Maxwell. The agreement was for Manley to catch wild horses for him, to pay for it. He brought him around one hundred head and then finished paying in cash for what was left owed.

One day on a June afternoon in 1867 about seven years after they were married, Manley and Theresa were coming toward Raton Pass where it was the narrowest through the canyon. There was a gate across the road, and a man came from the adobe house just beyond the gate. It was Richens Lacy Wootton, better known as 'Uncle Dick Wootton.' He had set the road up with the gate and was calling it his 'toll road.' Manley paid him a dollar for his wagon, and fifty cents for all extra horses and cows. 'Uncle Dick' then invited them in for supper and to spend the night so they stayed.

During their conversation the subject of Indians came up, and Uncle Dick told him about some trouble in Trinidad, but Lucien sent for Kit (this was reminiscent of the days before Kit died), and Kit powwowed with them, and Lucien gave the Indians twenty five ponies and all was well. As far as them bothering in their area he told them "Just set out a bucket of milk and some loaves of bread and they will leave you alone. "They followed his advice!

Now late in the fall of 1867 Goodnight was driving a herd north again by way of his and Loving's trail, but deviated a little bit this time to make it shorter. He pointed the herd northeastward, toward the Capulin Vega, where a remnant herd from past fall was being held. He gathered up and combined the two herds, turning northwest toward Raton Pass which was the gateway between New Mexico and Colorado. They went across the high country and started up the Raton Range where it passed over the divide and dropped down on the Colorado side. The outfit came to a halt, guess where? Yep! Uncle Dick Wootton's toll gate. He told them ten cents for every animal to continue their drive. Goodnight protested as he thought the toll was too high. Uncle Dick did not waver and Goodnight swore that if he did not reduce his price that he would find another pass and blaze a new trail. Wootten laughed in his face.

At the Apishapa forty miles northeast of Trinidad, Colorado that lay at the head of a canyon where Goodnight established a cattle ranch, he turned the cattle loose and left some of his hired hands to ride herd on the cattle and build a log cabin and then he returned to help Joe Loving, that was at the partnership ranch holding his herd. Joe was only twenty one years old and just a might young to handle the thirty two hundred head he had started trailing. Goodnight then helped him after he lost one thousand head of his herd, by taking one thousand of the best ones and leaving him there with the rest of the herd Goodnight returned to the Apishapa with that part of the herd. He then rode back to Fort Sumner, arriving in February.

His next drive up, he went east fifty miles of Loving's first trip then passed just west of Capulin, and went down to Cimarron Seco, then turned up the South Trinchera to cross the Raton Pass, a full two days east of Wootton's. He had kept his word about finding a new pass.

In April, the spring of 1869 Joel and John were trailing a herd of sixteen hundred head of cattle across the divide between Cherry Creek and the Bijou, according to the 'Pueblo Chieftan', "they were attacked by a gang of marauders estimated to number about fifty".

These men shot and killed quite a number of the cattle, and wounded many others. They stampeded the entire herd, claiming they feared Texas fever, but the paper affirmed that their object was 'doubtless plunder'. By 'Texas Fever' they were referring to 'Tick Fever', a disease that cattle get. The Texas Longhorns were immune to it but carriers of it. The domestic cattle of other States were not immune to it, and when a herd of Texas cattle came through certain states, their cattle would get sick and die because of it. There was a lot of fighting, almost wars over the problem.

At the time of the attack on the herd, Joel and John were trailing behind Frank Pope who had just passed through from Taos country,and he sent back for re–enforcements, and made plans with about thirty men, to take his herd of twelve hundred on, by fighting, if necessary.

For awhile there had been an organization in Fremont, Arapahoe, Boulder and El Paso Counties called 'The Colorado Cattle Association' and their object was to keep this kind of stock from going close to the settlements. These men had pledged that none of the Texas herds would pass over the main thoroughfare between the Arkansas and Platte River, unless they had been at least one year within the limits of the Territory.

Goodnight diverted his trail to the east of the troubled areas, and was able to continue his drives without any serious conflicts. When this came up between the association and the drovers, the men from the association of El Paso and Douglas counties made a reply to the '*Pueblo Chiefton*' by saying, "The Texans were attempting to force passage through the most thickly settled portions of both counties, after being asked to go around 'on a perfectly feasible route,' where they would not come in contact with American cattle, nor graze on their range." They also claimed "The Texans defiled us, saying they would drive, 'where they '*blankety*' well pleased."

Later a test case was taken to court alleging that the quarantine law was an invasion of the rights of Congress, and in the fall of 1870 'the Denver newspapers,' so Pueblo observed ' made quite a parade of a judicial decision' by the Second Districts judge 'to the effect that the law is unconstitutional and void.' The real joke of this decision was, when it came to knowledge that the law in question was never enforced in the Territory, and was repealed by the last Legislature....'

After some time went by, Theresa had a little girl named Lottie and on April 26, 1870 they had a son that they named after one of Manley's brothers, George Mason, and they called him 'Mason'. Mason is an interest here because he eventually became the husband of a granddaughter of Joel. Her name was Henrietta after her grandmother but was known as

Nettie. She was fifteen years old when they married and he was twenty four but they seemed to be completely happy and strangely suited to each other. She was a robust, outgoing girl, as likely to be out helping the men, as in their neat little house.

Manley had never paid much attention to her before; she was just one of the Curtis girls but now that he looked at her he liked her frank eyes, quick smile and enthusiasm. He and Theresa come to love her very much and she made Mason a wonderful wife.

In the writings that came from Zenus's family, Mary Todhunter Curtis, Zenus's wife and their children were in a wagon going to one of the hoe downs they enjoyed. Zenus played the fiddle and was already at the place they were going. A storm came up suddenly and lightening hit near the wagon. Nettie was wearing a gold bead necklace and the lightening was so intense that it melted the beads in her skin and were imbedded there until she died.

Nettie Curtis Chase

Henrietta 'Nettie' or 'Net' 'Curtis' Chase

Nettie was the daughter of Zenus and Mary Curtis

On July 17, 1870 Joel and his family were enumerated in the census in Elizabeth City, Colfax County, New Mexico. Sometime between the census of June 8, 1880 and a letter written by Tom to some of the family in 1898, Tscharner was not mentioned, and does not show up in any more census reports. So during the years of 1880 where he was enumerated and stated that he was fourteen, and 1998 when Tom wrote the letter, he must have died.

In 1871 and 1872 Joel was listed on the school tax list in Raton, Colfax County, and recorded the Maxwell land deed in the office of Louis E. Armijo, on July 18, 1871.

John's cousin, Dick Miller's sister, married Tom Maulding, and Lavinia having come into this large family, soon learned about everyone, and took charge, making a home for John and his boys.

Left: Mason Chase, husband of Nettie and one of his friends, John Land (1892) Mason was the son of Manley and Theresa Chase

In December of 1872 Henrietta had a baby girl. They named her Louann D. Curtis but called her 'Lula' and the same month, shortly after she was born, Henrietta died from complications of child birth, and was buried in the Dawson Cemetery. This left Joel with nine children, the ninth being a new born.

The older boys of Joel and Henrietta were now being schooled by Aunt Lavinia, as were some of the other children of the families around them, but the smaller children had to be looked after. Thomas and Luzan, as they had done for John, now stepped up and took charge of the small ones.

Joel was again on the school tax list in 1873, in Raton, Colfax County, and on June 3, 1873 he married Rosalina Emily White.

Also In 1873 the cattlemen that were associated together through the years had several different cattle companies and these same men, Tom Maulding, Manley Chase, Joel Curtis, and John B. Dawson, were the nucleus of the Board of Directors of said companies. Manley did not claim to be a market trader, but was a livestock man, who raised steers, and then arranged with John to trail them to the markets. Manley also kept the books.

Rosalina was the daughter of John Godfrey and Parshana A. 'Bailey' White. John White was born December 15, 1820 and died January 10, 1889 in Lincoln County, New Mexico and is buried in the Peñasco cemetery near Mayhill, New Mexico.

Parshanna was born December 27, 1820 in Mississippi, and she died December 12, 1896 in Arkansas. There is no true information on where she was buried, some think that she was buried by her husband but not for sure. John and Parshanna were married February 6, 1851 and Rosalina was born June 23, 1859 in Alabama.

As I was growing up I remember my dad telling me that our folks, named White, owned a mine at Trinidad, Colorado but I never really found out who it was for sure, and as a kid, I wasn't so much interested in 'that kind of stuff' but now I wish I had asked more about it.

Papers were found on Family History, (research assistance for the State of New Mexico), for 'The Primitive Baptist Church' for the year 1874, indicating that a church was formed. The group met at G.E. Millers house to organize a predestinarian Baptist church and a sermon was preached by Mr. T. R. Rule called 'Elder Rule'. The church was constituted and the nine constituents were received and named faithful to the order, as held by the old school Baptist. The signed "Brethren" Were G.E. Miller Sr., G.E. Miller Jr., J.G. White, J.W. Curtis, T.H. Dawson, P.A. White, Luann J.B. Dawson, Catharine K. Miller, and Lavinia J. Dawson. Here I have a question? Luann and J.B. Dawson are run together. Should not there have been a camma between Luann and J. B. Dawson which would have made ten people that were constituted?

After John Dawson and Lavinia had John B. Dawson Jr., and the reformation came to the valley, instead of having him Christened, as they had done with the older children, at the ancient two hundred and fify year old Catholic church of St. John between Ocate and Springer, New Mexico, they had him Christened in a new building, built near Maxwell, by the Baptist Church.

Some more uneasy days for the valley were going on during the year 1874.

Harry, a negro man working for the Chases, the only hand at the home place, was beaten over the head with sticks by three Indians. Theresa opened the door as he ran for it and she had a rifle in hand and gave Harry a pistol. The Indians made some belligerent signs toward them and shot some arrows into the air but eventually went into the brush along the river. They realized that the Indians had been drinking. Someone was selling the Indians liquor.

Manley was furious at whoever was doing this. He had the Sheriff call a town meeting. Between fifteen to ten men came and Manley talked to them about 'The Government needing to control the situation by making it a federal offense to sell liquor to the Indians. He also felt that the Indians should be given permanent suitable land so they could live better by having cattle and a place to hunt and fish or even farm if they wanted to. He also thought that they should try to keep the peace until the government acted.

The group all agreed and made a resolution that anyone selling liquor to the Indians: their supplies would be destroyed and anyone hiding information about said discrimination would be made to leave town within forty eight hours.

One week after the meeting when the Indians came to the mill on ration day, a fight broke out between the Apaches and Utes. Knives and arrows were used, but no guns. An Apache was killed by a Ute, and the next day, in retaliation, an Apache killed the Ute. When ration day came up the following week they all showed up painted, armed and ready for a showdown. Coming face to face in front of the mill the Utes demanded to take the life of the Apache that had killed their comrade but, of course, were refused. People scattered, fearing for their lives but the agent talked both sides into taking ten days rations and go back to their respective camps. During their return to the mountains the Apaches were ambushed by the Utes and they killed the one they had asked for.

The government was not controlling the situation and Manley was again talking to all those that would listen. The troubles seemed to be wide spread all over the country.

The news was everywhere even by word of mouth.

Stories were spreading throughout the once peaceful valley that there were uprisings in the Dakotas where Custer's Army was wiped out.

They were hearing that thousands of Cheyenne, Arapaho, Comanche, and Kiowa were getting together on the plains for a buffalo hunt but there were groups in small numbers, leaving the main bunch and attacking all over, even in eastern Colfax County. A report came from Colorado, that along Trinchera Creek, twelve people had been killed.

A very early photo possibly at the time of their marriage (1873) and a later photo of Joel W. and Rosalina 'White' Curtis

The day came when the peaceful valley was in the fray. A boy rode into Manley's place out of breath and riding hard. The horse was sweating and tired and the boy was shouting "Indians!" "Indians!" Some Kiowa and

Cheyenne had attacked some cowboys on the Vermejo, northeast about twelve miles up. Manley and Ed McBride plus two of their hands grabbed their guns and left immediately. They were worried about the Dawsons and others that were working in the pastures on the Vermejo. Also Manley's Uncle Milton had moved there and built a cabin approximately seven miles up Chase Canyon. He was supposed to be working with some of the work hands that day. They found that the settlers had not been in the attack but the cowboys working in the high country caught it. Milt's partner had been killed and Milt had a bullet graze his head. Milt's partner was Nicholson and they were working with the herd, and Milt was riding toward them when he saw the Indians headed toward Nicholson. He thought at first they were some of the home Indians, but when they started shooting he knew they were in trouble. They killed Nicholson the first thing and then shot Milt. He was able to hang on his horse and rode to the Dawson's place without them following and that is where Manley found him and learned what happened. John told Manley "They were just after the horses, not Milt."

I wonder if during these raids was when Joel lost the cattle that he filed on for reimbursement of the government. It seemed here, however, they were only taking horses and I realize also that it could have been while they were still in Texas as the Cheyenne and Kiowa were raiders in both Texas and here, at this time. Either way there were a lot of herds, both cattle and horses that were being taken by the Indians throughout a lot of years as the country was being settled by the white people.

The boy, in the mean time, that had sounded the alarm rode on to Cimarron, at Manley's command, to get help and when they arrived at the Dawsons they found the trail but the raiders had too much of a head start on them. As they followed the trail, they heard the same stories from the people on all the places they came to, but they never caught up with the Indians. They heard later that the stolen horses and the thieves had gone down Crow Creek killing two other herders and taking their horses also. They then went north, killing Uncle Dick Wooten's herder at his ranch and took his herd, then disappeared in the mountains.

The soldiers from Fort Union showed up in pursuit of them so the men from Cimarron returned home. From then on, for a time, the Indians continued attacking and killing whatever and whoever they could find as they rode all across the country. Wagon trains, freighters, sheep camps and settlers cabins all fell under their rampages. The soldiers kept after them all the way to the plains but never caught them.

The folks all around Cimarron and the outlying towns were on edge and afraid for sometime, even the work and other things being done were slowed to an uneasy pace and everyone had their guns handy for quick use if necessary. Several months passed and the raiders did not return. Things slowly went back to normal.

Normal was short lived though, because in late summer there were disagreements over the Maxwell Land Grant. Violence broke out once again in the valley, but this time between the people that lived here. There were a lot of people killed, a lot of enemies made of what used to be friends, over the disagreements and in 1875 it was building to a violent climax.

This was cause for John Dawson eventually ending up in a very heated court battle over his land with the Maxwell Land Grant Company. Dawson was eventually proved "not guilty" conclusively, and the plaintiff had to pay all court costs.

John was now sixty three and had just won a tough court battle. He was not "old" in having bad health or 'spunk' but he had been a lot of miles. He was now appreciative of the kindness of his circle of friends and family. The work of taking care of his place and family settled back to a proper way of living.

The valley was once again booming and people were prospering only from the sweat of their brow and smart business practices.

On March 24, 1875 Joel's daughter, Alvia Curtis married William T. Mathews, in Colfax County, and on April 12, 1875 Joel sold all of his land, except for the home place, to John Dawson. The deed was recorded in book A, page 403 in Raton, Colfax County.

From all of the disasters of losing his horses and cattle to the Indians and the loss of a couple of children and then the loss of Henrietta, and being left with small children to raise, I'm sure this was disheartening for Joel and maybe that is why he sold his interest in the land to John, just retaining his home and a small plot around it, for him and his new wife to have a place to live.

Rosalina had very beautiful features and was twenty days away from being fifteen years old. Joel certainly had an eye for beauty. He had turned fifty five but was still in his prime. He was a tough, hardened cowboy, 'cattle drover' and horseman, Indian fighter, exTexas Ranger, defender of the frontier, and had been married for twenty four years to another woman whom he had loved dearly and had nine children by her, the youngest only six months old.

Did Rosa know what kind of life she was getting into? I think she did, but back then there were very few people in these parts of the country and most of the good steady men were taken. There were a lot of drifters and wild crazy men like Clay Allison that quiet, more refined girls stayed clear of when looking to marry. Most girls married very young and had large families, so she was probably not intimidated by his children or his age. She must have seen a strong, tough man that took care of his family and made them a good living by hard work, honesty and moral practices.

On June 17, 1875, a month after the sale of the land, Rosalina had their first child, Hardin Wills Curtis.

Hardin had black hair like her mother and the same face structure.

In 1876 John Curtis married Elizabeth T. Turyman and on January 18, 1877 Frank married Melissa Ellen Mathews.

On April 4, 1877 Joel and Rosa had another baby girl and they named her Naomai Annie Curtis. This baby girl also had her mothers features. The girl descendants of Joel and both of his wives were all very pretty.

On August 7, 1878 Zenus married Mary Francis Todhunter, the girl that won his heart back during his school days. They were married at J.B. Dawson's ranch house on the Vermejo and John gave them a team of horses and a wagon for their wedding present.

On February 22, 1879 Rosa had her only son, Antonio Malush Curtis. He was called Tony or T.M. all of his life. The story was told to me that the name Malush was the name of an Indian friend of Joel's. On June 8, 1880 census Joel's family was enumerated in Raton, Colfax County, New Mexico.

There is information that tells that John G. White came to Lincoln County, previous to Joel, in 1878.

This could be why Joel chose to move to this location.

My Grandfather 'Tony' related to me that he was about two years old when they moved to Lincoln County in a covered wagon.

Joel settled on a one hundred and sixty acre homestead on the Peñasco River in Lincoln County Territory and it was stated in a news article that

Joel had settled here in 1880 so it must have been in the fall of that year before Tony turned two in February of 1881.

One year later Rosa delivered a baby girl on October 18, 1881, in Lincoln County Territory on the Upper Peñasco, New Mexico. They named her Norah "Nora" O. Jane Curtis. Some papers that we have says Jane was one of her names and then others never show up with it as part of her name, and no one knows what the O. stands for.

First residence built in present day Mayhill, NM which was then called Upper Penasco, Territory of New Mexico. The dwelling still existed in 1995 and was occupied.

From the right: two girls unknown, Albert M. Coe, (soninlaw of John Mahill), unknown girl, Mollie Mahill Coe, (wife of Albert). Sarah Paggitt Mahill, (wife of John Mahill), the two small children are unknown. John Mahill is in the white shirt and standing near window, others are unknown. Circa 1882. Courtesy of Elizabeth (Beth) Mahill

The first residence built in the town that was later called Mayhill was built in 1882 and a photo appearing in 'A Pictorial History of Otero County, New Mexico' book had John Mahill and some of his family in front of it. The town of 'Mayhill' was named after the Mahill family but was misspelled and never changed to the correct spelling. Thus with one house, a few more were added and soon a store, so a town was born. The first people that settled on the land that was eventually called Mayhill were Albert M. and Mollie 'Mahill' Coe in 1881, a year after Joel and Rosalina settled on the Upper Peñasco, three miles west of where Mayhill is now.

On February 28, 1882, Joel and Henrietta's oldest son 'Dick' married Martha Errie Brackett in Colfax county, New Mexico, in a cousins home, and on November 13th of that same year Rosa had another daughter and they named her Rosa V. Curtis. I'm not sure and have no proof but I think the V. could have been for Vivan. Nora and Rosie' were very close all through the years and when Nora had her first daughter she named her Vivan so I tend to think that she named her after her sister. On all papers and documents of Rosa V., she never put a name other than V. "Rosie" as everyone called her, was also born on the Peñasco place. Rosie was eighteen months old and on May 17, 1884 Rosalina passed away. I feel like Parshanna helped to raise these young children while she was alive. Hardin would have been nine, Naomi seven, Tony five, Nora was about three and the baby Rosie' one Year and five Months. I know that back in those days the older children had to take on pretty big loads and I'm sure, in my own mind, that Hardin and Naomi had to help with the younger children.

Joel continued to raise cattle and I'm sure that he taught Tony everything he could about cattle and running a place of his own. It is possible he may have farmed some too just to have their vegetables to eat and some to sell or trade, and to raise feed for his horses and cattle for the winter months. Tony busted broncs for a living when he was a young man but after he married he worked on the home place.

Joel's father–in–law, was there with Joel and Rosa, and Probably helped with the ranch as much as possible until he passed away on January 10, 1889. John White was buried close to Rosa in the Peñasco Cemetery, Mayhill, New Mexico.

There is no way of knowing how many of Joel's older children, from Henrietta, moved with them to Lincoln County but evidently Joel the Third was with them for he died in 1885, just one year after Rosalina died and is also buried near the family in Lincoln County in the Peñasco Cemetery, Mayhill, New Mexico.

The cemetery on the Peñasco has two parts to it. Some say that part of it is under the hill but my description is that the old part where Joel,

Rosalina, Joel the third, John White and others of the first pioneers were buried beside the hill, next to the road and later generations were buried on top of the hill on a mesa. It is all fenced in and there is a metal gate that is kept locked to keep it protected. It is about one mile out of Mayhill on the Peñasco River road.

Lincoln County in the early 1850's was still wild. The Mescalero Apaches were upset over all the homesteaders that were invading their world and the U.S. Government was having a lot of trouble trying to maintain peace. The Indians were raiding the homesteads and stealing horses, cattle and sheep in order to survive as the white settlers were killing the wild game also to survive. The settlers, because of their fear of the raiders, asked for the help of the military.

Captain Henry W. Stanton for whom Fort Stanton was named, and a troop of soldiers came from San Patricio to try to squelch the problem. They were traveling up the Rio Peñasco on January 18, 1855 when the Indians surprised them and Stanton among several others, were killed. The killing happened in the vicinity of present day Mayhill. There was a marker in the town that recorded this historical Incident, but I'm not sure it is still there.

Mayhill is on the eastern slopes of the Sacramento Mountains and is located at the forks of the Rio Peñasco and James Canyon about seventeen miles east of Cloudcroft on U.S. Highway 82 by way of James Canyon. If traveling out of Cloudcroft on Cox Canyon then it is a little further and by going Cox Canyon to the Rio Peñasco you will come to the junction going to Weed.

In 1867, a man named Albert Coe had come to New Mexico along with his brother Frank and cousin George. Frank and George became involved with Billy the Kid and the Lincoln County Wars and Albert came to the Rio Peñasco area in 1873 . He settled on what I knew as the Jimmy Mahill Ranch about half a mile east of the town of Mayhill. One of the log cabins he built was still standing on the old homestead the last time I was in Mayhill.

Other settlers a few year later were listed: Charles Arthur (1884), Teen Clayton (1883), John Gardessler (1880), Joel Warner Curtis (1880), Ben Henry (1882), Alfred and Kim Hunter (1884), John James (1879), Henry Kepler (1884), Robert McGee (1878), W.C. Warren (1878), and John G. White (1878).

Albert Coe returned to his former home in Missouri, in 1881 to marry his childhood sweetheart, Mary "Mollie" Mahill and they returned to his homestead on the Rio Peñasco. John and Sara Mahill and their family, Mollie's parents, joined them one year later.

Mollie 'Mahill' Coe was the first Post Misteress in Mayhill and the Post Office was in the Coe home.

John James was the first to own the spot that is now called Mayhill and all the surrounding area and it was he that James Canyon was named for. He sold all this land for three hundred dollars to John Mahill in December of 1882 and John built an adobe house that, as far as I know, is still standing and occupied. It was the first house built in Mahill.

On May 1, 1885 a family by the name of Brantley left Llano County, Texas with their three children and headed west. Fredrick "Fred" Brantley had married Sarah Jane Doggett on July 4, 1878 in Hamilton County, Texas. Sarah was the daughter of Ebenezer and Elizabeth 'Bearden' Doggett and her siblings included Mary called 'Nat', John, Mansel, Bob, Charley and Cleatus.

Sarah was born January 18, 1863 in Red River County, Texas and Fredrick was born July 30, 1860 in Burnet County, Texas, to Joseph Josiah and Elizabeth Mariah 'Grosbeck ' Brantley. Two of his brothers were Hiram 'Hite' T. and Oscar (Preston Brantley, one of the researchers for the Brantley family told me that Hite and Oscar were half brothers).

Josiah was a Jr. as in the 1830 Greene County, Illinois census there is Josiah Brantley age between 50 and 60, Married to Nancy age 50 to 60 and children listed as Henry B. born 1800 and married 1832 shows his wife to be Nancy born 1806 and married 1831 so not sure which date is right for their marriage. The other child listed is Josiah Jr. born 1812 married August 1830 and his wife has a question mark, then Elizabeth married 1834 or Elizabeth' Whitaker', wife of Josiah Jr. ?

Josiah C. Brantley was Born about 1772 or 73 in Edgecombe County, North Carolina and his father was John Brantley Jr. 1730 to 1786. Date of Josiah's death is given as 1857 in Bastrop County, Texas and is buried at the Lower Cedar Creek Cemetery in Bastrop County, Texas. A census timeline for him is 1800, Nash County, North Carolina. 1820, Russelville, Logan County, Kentucky. 1830, Greene County, Illinois. 1835, Morgan County, Illinois. 1840, Red River County, Texas. He married Nancy (maiden name unknown) in 1794 (possibly in Edgecombe County, North

Carolina). Seven children were found for them as follows: James Perry was born in 1795 in North Carolina and he married Sarah Whitaker on 18 July 1822 in Logan County, Kentucky . Temperance 'Tempey' was born in 1797 in North Carolina and Married Archibald Davis on 19 August 1817 in Logan County Kentucky, I have no knowledge of what happened to Archibald but she married again to Mark Whitaker on 5 May 1824 in Logan County Kentucky. Henry was born in 1800 in North Carolina and married Agnes Chipman 1 November 1832 in Morgan County Illinois. Martha D. was born 14 February 1803 in North Carolina and married James B. Carr on 15 September 1824 in Logan County Kentucky. Nancy was born on 6 November 1806 in Mercer County, Kentucky and she married James Blair. Elizabeth was born 1809 in Kentucky and married Ira Clark on 19 June 1834 in Morgan County, Illinois.

Josiah Jr. was born 1812, in Kentucky and married Elizabeth Whitaker 26 August 1830 in Green County, Illinois. I'm not sure but I think Elizabeth died and then he married Mariah Groesbeck some time before the 1850 census, in Bastrop County, Texas. It is not known at this time, but there possibly were more children.

The eight identified families of the interrelated group that moved to Texas were: James B. Carr and his wife Martha Brantley Carr: James F. Whitaker and his wife Anna: James Blair and his wife Nancy Brantley Blair: Josiah Brantley Jr. and his wife Elizabeth Whitaker: Josiah Brantley Sr. and his wife Nancy: Henry Brantley and his wife Agnes Chipman Brantley: James P. Brantley and his wife Sarah Whitaker Brantley: Francis Winans and his wife Julia Ann Whitaker.

There are probably other families of Carr Brantley–Whitaker relationship that moved in that loose association from North Carolina to Kentucky to Illinois to Red River County, Texas. In subsequent years the Carrs and some of the Blairs moved west following the frontier; but many of the Brantleys and Whitakers moved south to Bastrop following James Brantley.

From a writing, 'History of Texas…Tarrant & Parker Counties'; A Biographical sketch of William H. Carr, Pgs 476478, Chicago, Illinois., Lewis Publishing company, 1895.

William H. Carr, Aledo, Texas was one of the prosperous farmers and stock dealers of Parker County. A sketch of his life is herewith presented:

William H. Carr was born in Scott County, Illinois, January 12, 1834, son of J.B. and Martha (Brantley) Carr, the former a native of North Carolina, and the latter of Kentucky. They went to Illinois at an early day, and first settled in Greene County, from whence they subsequently removed to Scott County, the birthplace of William H. In 1846 the Carr family emigrated to Texas, and located in Red River County, thence removed to Collin County, and in July, 1855, came to Parker County, and settled on a farm on Clear Fork Creek, where the father was engaged in farming and stockraising the rest of his life, and where he died, in 1874, at the age of seventy six years, his wife surviving him until 1876. He was a veteran of the Black Hawk war. His ancestors were Irish, while the Brantleys originated in England. Grandfather Josiah Brantley came from Illinois to Texas in 1840, and located in Red River County. He subsequently removed to Bastrop County, where he died at the age of eighty five years. All his life he was a farmer and stockraiser. The names of J.B. and Martha Carr's children are as follows: Emily E., who married E. Gaither; Calvin M.; Henry: William H., whose name heads this article; Temperance, wife of John Blackwell; Mary: James: and Martha, wife of Fate Blackwell, all deceased except three, Henry, William H., and James.

Mr. Carr was always a Union man. When the war broke out he entered the State service, and was on the frontier of Texas protecting the settlers from the depredations of the Indians until the war closed. During the time he was a ranger he and others of this command visited the spot where Wichita Falls is now located. He is said to have been the first white man who stood on that ground. That was August 7, 1863.

The place of birth and ancestry for William H. Carr was taken from the tombstone inscription and is accepted here, but it is noted that the Wm. H. Carr bio says James B. died in 1874 at age 76 which would place his birthdate in 1797 or 1798. Regarding Irish ancestry, there were indeed Carrs in Ireland. Records of the 'Parish Registry Society of Dublin' for 1636–1700 contain 27 individual listings having Carr as the family name. Given names included James, William, Elizabeth, Thomas, John, and Mary which are recurring names in this Carr history nearly 200 hears later although there is no known connection to the Dublin Carrs. Also, some Carr families in the U.S. trace their ancestry to the Scottish "Kerr" clan. Carr is also known to be an English place name approximately meaning "the low ground" and the Carr's were all the people living down there.

This is a story told by Preston Brantley and typed by his wife Jeanne. It is about James Perry, Josiah's older brother.

Perry and The New Mexico Campaign:

As I start this portion of family history I can't help but wonder where Perry died. Following the Confederate through the New Mexico Campaigns during the Civil War I wonder where he died. Was it a battle up through the Rio Grande Valley, was it at Glorietta, or on the long march home from El Paso to San Antonio? I don't think the family ever knew because grandpa had expressed a wish to go to "Mexico" and find Perry. I do know this was another sorrow for Josiah Jr. The son who never came home.

Jeanne then put this poem at the end of this note:

When all my questions are answered
From God who can answer all
Perhaps I could humbly ask him
Where did Perry fall
But then it really won't matter
For the long hard marches are done
The last battle on earth has ended
The final battle won.

Jeanne's final paper from Preston's words on Perry:

Perry Brantley 'The New Mexico Campaign'

I first heard of Perry, my grandfather Fred's brother one day when I was a small boy. Grandpa stood gazing at the hills surrounding his New Mexico ranch as if he saw something beyond his line of vision.

"I'd like to go to Mexico and see if I could find Perry," he said.

"Who is Perry?" I asked. "he is my older brother, and he never came back from the war" he answered.

Now I wish that I had asked more but like most children my interests involved the present more than the past so I left the old man to his reminiscening and like many lost opportunities I never learned more from him. Through the years his conversation remained a shadow in my memory and when I began my family history I started documenting the war records of Perry.

50

His name was James (probably for his uncle James) Perry Brantley, son of Josiah Brantley and Elizabeth Whitaker Brantley, the second son of that couple. At the age of twenty seven he joined Sibley's Texas Volunteers and served under Captain John Phillip's Brigade. Like most young men he could have had no conception of the hardships and sorrows that would follow Sibley's dream of capturing New Mexico for the Confederacy.

Leaving San Antonio the army made the long journey to El Paso where Sibley set up his temporary command post on December 14th 1861. Even today with our fast mode of travel and comforts we enjoy while traveling this is a long lonesome stretch of country, so I can well imagine how difficult their journey was.

Perry had supplied his own horse, saddle and gun, as was required, and I'm sure that father Josiah saw that he was suitably mounted for his great adventure.

When General Sibley established his temporary headquarters at El Paso and assumed command of all Confederate forces in Texas at Ft. Quitman and the territories of New Mexico and Arizona, Perry was there.

I find Captain John Phillips brigade mentioned as the Confederates that left El Paso and moved up the Mesilla Valley, preparing to engage General Canby's Union forces in the battle for New Mexico.

Perry's records from the National Archives show that Perry was never paid for his military service but that was not unusual since Sibley had no money to pay the troop most of the time, and had very little for supplies. A great part of the time the men were forced to rely on captured bounty and live off the land's sparse resources. Cold and hungry they, never the less, pressed on toward Albuquerque.

I am not mentioning the various battles that took place for this can be read by any one who is interested in history, but I will say that I find Phillips Brigade to be present through the entire campaign and can only speculate as to Perry's fate. Whether he died early or late I will never know for John Philips muster records were lost.

If Perry did survive the retreat to El Paso after the final defeat at Glorietta, and the subsequent return to San Antonio there is no record.

When grandpa told me he always wanted to go to Mexico to find Perry, I am sure he was remembering that his folks told him that Perry never returned from the war in Mexico. Even now some people confuse

New Mexico and probably the New was dropped from the conversation and all his life he thought Perry fought in Mexico.

Being unfamiliar with history of the New Mexico Campaign I can't help but think how amazed he would have been to realize that when he settled in New Mexico he was not too far from the places where Perry fought and probably died.

I have no record of a marriage for Perry but I will continue to search and perhaps some day I may even discover his descendants, if he had any.

After this was written a write up on Vigo Park, Texas, page 843 on the Village Creek, Battle Of. From a Bibliograpy: Walter G. Cook, "The Battle of Village Creek," Junior Historian, V (1944–1945): Rex Wallace Strickland, "History of Fannin County, Texas, 1836–1843," Southwestern Historical Quarterly, XXXIV (1930–1931); Monuments Erected....to Commemorate the Centenary of Texas Independence (1939). The piece written is this: Village Creek, Battle of. The battle of Village Creek occurred on May 24, 1841, along Village Creek in Tarrant County. A force of approximately seventy men, including Texas Rangers, under the command of General Edward H. Tarrant, took two Indian Villages without much difficulty, but a third village, having been informed of the impending attack, put up resistance. After the third village was taken, two patrols of ten men each were sent out under the command of Captains John B. Denton and William H. Bourland. Drawn into a trap, the Texans suffered considerable losses and Denton was killed. Bourland was able to return to the encampment, and General Tarrant made an orderly retreat with Indian Booty. As a result of this raid, the Indians migrated westward and establishment of Bird's Fort was made possible. A monument to Commemorate the battle was erected three miles east of Handley, Tarrant County, in 1936.

Some of the family has stated that this could be where James Perry was killed. About seventy eight men were there and about half were killed but there were no names given.

I have a copy of a probate settlement for James Brantley and this is a part of it: John Hobbs presented an account against the Estate of James Brantly, Decd., for the sum of $4.56, which was allowed by the Court and ordered to be paid out of the effects of said Decd.

Jesse Billingsly petitioned the Court praying to be appointed guardian for Monroe Brantly, Minor Heir of James Brantly, Decd.

Whereupon consideration of the Court, it is Ordered and Decreed that Letters of Guardianship issue to the said Jesse Billingsly and, upon his giving Bond & Security according to Law.

And it is further Ordered that said Billingsly retain the amount of money in his hands belonging to the Succession of James Brantly, Decd., for the benefit of said Minor Heir.

Desha Bunton petitioned the court to be appointed Guardian for Mary Brantly, Minor Heir of James Brantly, Decd.

Whereupon consideration of the Court it was Ordered and Decreed that Desha Bunton be appointed Guardian as aforesaid.

Desha Bunton was a close relative of President Lyndon Johnson.

There was speculation made that this could have been where one of Fred's sons, Monroe, got his name.

Josiah Jr's brother Henry is listed in the 1835 Green County, Illinois State census as age thirty to forty and is married to an Agnes and a child named Ebeneser born 1835 and Agnes had a child Polly born 1833.

In The Illinois State Historical Library, Springfield 1970, volume xxxv on The Black Hawk War of 1831–1832 (volume I of Illinois Volunteers), Page 374, Josiah is listed as a private out of Green County, Illinois on their muster roll under Captain Aaron Barrow's Company, second regiment, third brigade of the Illinois Mounted Volunteers called into the service of the United States on the requisition of General Atkinson by the Governor's proclamation, dated the fifteenth of May, 1832. This company organized & C., in White Hall Green County Illinois the fifth of June, 1832. On page 375 it continues with names and then statements are made below. "I do certify on honor that this campaign furnished themselves with forage for their horses during the campain, and themselves with provisions for 10 days and that no officer in this Company have drawn but one Ration per day and all the statements within inserted are correct. Given under my hand at Fort Dixon fifteenth August, 1832, "signed: Aaron Barrow Capt.

A Record of Events, which may be useful to be noticed. This company was enrolled fifth June, 1832 and marched eighth day June to Fort Wilbourn where they were mustered into the service of the United States on nineteenth June, 1832.

Josiah Brantley was wounded July 2, 1832.

On page 222 under Company of Captain John Summers and Later Seth Pratt, Henry Brantley is also listed in the Black Hawk Campaign of 1832.

Mariah is found on the 1850 census as a minor in the household of Josiah Jr.. It is presumed that for some reason, Josiah had taken her into his household as a child. It was thought by someone that she might have been a niece but that was not proven. The date of their marriage is unknown.

There is a discrepancy in her birth date from old records. It stated she was born in 1814, but according to a census record, she was born in 1812. The old record showed her death date to be 1890 and she was buried in the James Canyon Cemetery.

Josiah was married another time to a lady who remains unknown. However it is known that they had two children named Mark and Lou.

When Fred and Sarah Brantley left Texas on May 1, 1885 they had three children with them: Alma Alice, 'Allie' as they called her, was five born February 15, 1880 in Llano County, Texas: Margaret Adelia, 'Maggie' as they called her, was three, born October 21, 1882 in Llano County, Texas: and Roy, 'Bud' as they called him, was one, born April 13, 1884, in Llano County, Texas.

Fred's parents, Josiah and Mariah went with them. Also Fred's brother Hiram, or 'Hite' as they called him, and his wife Bettie with their four children, Joseph 'Monk' age eight, Dee age six, Will age five, and Myrtle age three.

Myrtle married a man named John Evans on November 19, 1899 in an old log house she grew up in. They had five children, Lola born 1900, Gladys in 1902, Clifford in 1905 (deceased in childhood), Lawrence in 1907, and Jesse in 1909. They had eighteen grandchildren, fourteen great grandchildren, and three great, great grandchilddren.

Oscar, another brother of Fred's, went to New Mexico later. He was possibly sixteen years old when his parents started traveling west. He married Annie Holland and they had two children, Iva and Frank.

It took two months to make the trip in their wagons with teams of horses and oxen. They had a milk cow or two so the little ones could have fresh milk on the way. Bettie was ill in bed when they started on their journey. By the time they arrived in James Canyon, New Mexico where they settled, she was able to get into and out of the wagon.

Another traveler named Baird and five of his boys overtook them on the road and continued on the journey with them. When they arrived in James Canyon, Mr. Baird filed a claim on land that is near what later became known as the Wimsatt Store. There were other Bairds in the area: Tate Baird settled in Orr Canyon, Nat Baird at Pine Springs and there was a Baird homestead in the area that would later be known as Baird Canyon. It's possible that this was John Baird who was probably a brother to Tate and Nat. Hite and Bettie continued on down the Canyon and settled on land that was eventually called the Calentine Place.

The Brantley family 1904 or 05

Back row: Mark, Alice 'Allie', Allie's husband Hobson Clark, Margaret 'Maggie', Roy 'Bud'.

Front row: Lee, Fred, Monroe, Sarah, babyNola, Mary 'Mamie'

Jim Hunter (Jimmy Mahill's grandfather) settled in James Canyon, the year before the Brantleys, on what later became The Burgett Floral. They built several large hot houses and grew and shipped flowers everywhere during their years in business. Jim Hunter gave Bill Samons a shotgun for his claim.

All the men helped each other to get settled and make homes for the families. Some of them had to cut trees for log cabins. They had fire places and cook stoves but not much room in them. They managed to enjoy their lives, despite the hardships.

They got together and built a log church house and everyone went to church on Sundays. They took their dinner and stayed all day. The logs of the old church were still there for awhile but a new building was built along with a cemetery next to it. This church is still standing and is known as the James Canyon Church.

Fred filed on land in Eight Mile Canyon where he truck farmed for several years. He said when he settled he had fifty cents and he bought nails to make doors for their log cabin. The nails were square then instead of round like they are today.

The Brantley family about 1911:

Back row: Mary 'Mamie', Lee, Bettie

Front row: Mark, Nola, Fred, Sarah, Elza, Monroe

Mariah died the year following their arrival in New Mexico. She was taken to a doctor at the Indian Agency when she became ill as no other doctor was available and she died there, probably from pneumonia. She is buried in the Peñasco Cemetery, at Mayhill, New

Mexico, in the part that is by the road. After her death, Josiah made his home with Fred's family and with Hite's family. He died in 1890 and is buried in the James Canyon Cemetery. Matching grave stones mark their graves in the two cemeteries. However, there is a military headstone honoring Josiah beside her headstone even though he is not buried there.

The first work Fred found was splitting rails for people to fence their claims. While living on Eight Mile, five more children were born. Mark was born September 8, 1888, Monroe David born April 30, 1890, Mary 'Mamie' Lue born March 11, 1893, Lee Everett born April 16, 1895, and Bettie Elizabeth born July 15, 1897.

Bettie Brantley, Hite's wife, passed away at the Indian Agency also. She was taken to the Agency when she became ill as there were still no doctors near. Hite then lived with Myrtle and John after her death.

In 1898, Fred sold the homestead on Eight Mile Canyon to John Eddy and purchased a place, east of Mayhill on the lower Rio Peñasco River, from James 'Jim' Hunter that had quite a bit of land where Mayhill became a town and on farther down the Peñasco. This property had been homesteaded by Charles Arthur in 1891 and later sold to Henry Stearns from Central Falls, Rhode Island.

Mr. Stearns in turn sold it to Jim Hunter in the later part of the same year. Fred paid Jim Hunter the sum of three hundred dollars for the eighty acre homestead. Fred had brought his 7B brand from Texas and had it registered in New Mexico in 1895. Many years later, people will recall seeing the brand on the chimney of the house on the Peñasco River.

Fred started another truck farm here but also started about five acres in orchards. He grew Mostly apples but also had peaches, pears, cherries, plums, one mulberry tree and a lot of gooseberries which supplied the whole family. He had several cows that he kept on the forest land and always had a good horse to ride and his work horse team for plowing the land. He really enjoyed riding his horse, and checking on his cows.

There was a story he used to tell to the grandchildren that Geronimo and his followers that roamed the mountains near by would come to the tree edge across from his place and sit. Fred would wave to them and they would come down to his place and he would give them food. They never bothered him or his family.

After moving to the new place they had four more children. Robert was born on November 11, 1900 at Mayhill and died on November 11, 1911: Fredrick E. born October 14, 1903 and died November 23, 1903.

Nola Irue was born September 12, 1904, and Elza Hillard on October 14, 1908. Roy 'Bud' died when just a youngster, on November 1, 1901, seventeen years old.

The Brantleys were of the Christian faith, being faithful members of the church of Christ at Mayhill, New Mexico and they were good friends and neighbors. They were always there to lend a hand, whether it was because of illness, hard luck or just to be a good neighbor. Fred had a large barn built for his apple's and sold a lot of the very best apples anywhere in the country. He raised vegetables, corn, and had good hay crops that were all required for daily survival for that time. He Hauled the produce to El Paso, Texas, or Roswell, New Mexico, to sell it. A trip to El Paso would take about eight days.

Fred provided day work for many families who were less fortunate and treated everyone fairly. He was a strict disciplinarian who was loved and respected by his children and grandchildren. Grandma Sarah was a softer touch. She always had a soft lap, a hug and provided a good meal, usually topped off by a fresh fruit cobbler. I loved the gooseberry cobbler, my mouth would water when I smelled them and boy did she ever make good sauerkraut. I remember as a child seeing the large wooden barrel out by the back porch that she made it in, 'yummy 'is the word.

There were still hard times for these Pioneer families and their neighbors that had started migrating to this part of the country. It was four days to Roswell, New Mexico and eight days to El Paso, Texas. They Drove their wagons, and teams all this way to sell their produce, and on the return trip brought staples, household goods, or whatever was needed to survive.

Most of their food they raised and one great thing about this area was good grazing country for stock and produce such as cabbage, onions, carrots and potatoes grew very well here plus hay and alfalfa also was grown for the stock for the winter months.

Water was plentiful most of the time. With good rains and winter snow there were many creeks, rivers, and springs that ran all year round.

Most all of the settlers raised horses and had a few head of cattle plus many of them had sheep and goats but, as always, Mother Nature was not very kind at times.

Joel continued to live and care for his family the best he could and life went on.

On March 20, 1890 his daughter Luann married James Hanna in Colfax County, New Mexico and in June of that same year he was enumerated on the 1890 census, A special schedule of surviving soldiers, on The Upper Peñasco River, Lincoln County, New Mexico.

On April 1, 1891, Joel filed property, taxes of six hundred and forty eight dollars, on his homestead. By 1892 he was completely blind and things were turned around for him, for now his children had to look out for him.

There were stories told about him though. They never moved anything in the house, and he became accustomed to getting around the house very well. It was said many times by several of the folks that knew him that he had a special path to the creek and would walk down by himself and bring back a couple of buckets of water when they needed it. He tried to stay as active and independent as possible.

He was called Captain Joel by all of the acquaintances he made and my father told me that he fought during the Civil War but he wasn't sure where or when. He said he thought he was in the Cavalry. Joel must not have told much about himself to his children or grand children because none of them knew much about his past. Maybe his memories were too painful to recount or possibly he was just a private person.

On August 10, 1893 Naomi married Jesse Walter Weldy Sr., on the Upper Peñasco River, at the Curtis homestead. He was born in Lampasas, Texas on September 22, 1865. They had 13 children: First was Joel Warner Sr. born September 9, 1894 in Roswell, New Mexico, second one Albert Edwin born on March 28, 1897 at Mayhill and died young on October 28, 1915 and is buried at Mayhill. The Third child was Rebecca Jane and she was born July 3, 1898 at Mayhill. Number

John and Luann 'Lulu' 'Curtis' Todhunter.

John is the cousin of Mary 'Todhunter' Curtis

Lulu was the last child born to Joel W. and Henrietta 'Dawson' Curtis

Four child was George Washington and he was born on March 21, 1900 at Mayhill. The fifth child was Jesse Luke and he was born on March 4, 1902 at Mayhill and died a year later on July 9, 1903 at Mayhill. The sixth one was William Thomas that was born on October 7, 1903 at Mayhill. The seventh child was Earl Curtis and he was born December 4, 1905 at Mayhill. Number eight was Elsie Irean and she was born January 5, 1908 in Artesia, New Mexico and she died a year later on March 10, 1909 in Artesia. The ninth child was Mable Elizabeth and she was born on March 18, 1910 in Jumbo, Arizona. Number ten was Lisbon Ival that was born on July 13, 1912 in Mayhill. Number eleven was Jessie Walter Jr. and he was born January 5, 1915 in Dayton, Eddy County, New Mexico. Number twelve was Luease May and she was born Mayhill on February 4, 1918 and died on February 11, 1918 in Eddy County, New Mexico and was buried beside the road between Artesia and Carlsbad, New Mexico. The last child to born was Wildy Lee and he was born on January 1, 1921 in Carlsbad, New Mexico.

The family is very extensive and wide spread but they have a full family tree. I was never around the Weldy family much as they lived in Carlsbad most of my growing up years but I did find out that Aunt Naomi died in a house fire on December 26, 1951. Jesse Walter died on January 9, 1964 and they are both buried in Carlsbad, New Mexico.

A Post Office had been set up on the Upper Peñasco on August 25, 1884 and when neighbors or any of them went to get their mail they would take all mail and distribute it to all that had mail. The roads back in the mid and late 1800's and early 1900's were not much more than cow trails and only widened by teams pulling wagons on them. When it rained or snowed it was sometimes impossible to navigate on the roads because of the mud.

The Penasco Post Office was discontinued on March 4, 1902 and a new one established on that day in the small place they now call Mayhill.

Most people did not travel much then unless it was necessary and neighbors were always there for each other whether to deliver some one's mail or to help deliver a baby, or take care of a sick one. If their cows were calving, they were getting out crops, needed help of any kind, you could always count on your neighbor.

The winters could be very harsh and long. Sometimes it would snow so deep, according to my dad, that when he rode his horse to school some days the snow would be belly high on his horse. During times like these they had to make sure they had plenty of wood gathered to make it through the winter. They used cross cut saws and axes and the men of the family would go into the forest and fall trees. They would bring them back to their places in horse drawn wagons then chop and split them for the fireplaces and wood cook stoves. All of this had to be done in the summer months so the wood could dry out by the fall, along with all the other work that went on in raising crops and taking care of the live stock. These pioneers would get up while it was still dark and work until it got so dark they couldn't see anymore. I'm so very sure of one thing. No one during that time ever said "I'm bored".

On June 19, 1892 Hardin married Alfred Dashiell Wallace on the Upper Penasco. Hardin and Alfred had five children: The first was Frances Elizabeth that was born in 1893 in Raton, New Mexico. The second child was Clarence Alfred and he was born on July 26, 1894 in Raton. The third child was Ora Harden and she was born October 26, 1895 at Mayhill. Their third one was Floyd R. and he was born in 1901 in New Mexico and the last child was Jewell and she was born in 1905 at Mayhill.

Jesse and Naomi 'Curtis' Weldy. Naomi was the second child born to Joel W. and Rosalina Curtis

Alfred and Hardin 'Curtis' Wallace. Hardin was the first child born to Joel W. and Rosalina Curtis

That next year on, December 23, 1893, with the help of his two younger daughters, Joel filed for an increase in his war pension. He received twelve dollars a month after the increase on July 10, 1894.

On November 5, 1895 he received a patent on his land through the Homestead Act, and on April 13, 1896 he filed his property tax that was four hundred dollars.

On September 1, 1899 he wrote an affidavit on the birth of his living children that he had with Henrietta for the estate of Thomas Dawson, and on November 5th of that same year Norah married, William Gus Moore, on the Upper Peñasco.

On June 5, 1900 Joel was enumerated in the 1900 census on the Upper Peñasco, and On October 9, 1901 a power of Attorney was signed by Joel, to a Milo B. Stevens to ask for another pay increase on his war pension. On February 18, 1902 he received a certificate of pay still at twelve dollars a month. On May 4, 1902 he asked for a new certificate of pay because his daughters Nora and Rosa had lost or misplaced the one that had been sent.

Gus Moore and Norah had a son named Andrew and I have no date for his birth. I was told when Andrew was still very young that Gus Moore stole a cow and he took off, hearing the law was after him, never to be seen or heard from again.

There was a Man named David Dollins, and his son Melvin, that moved into the country between the summer of 1910 and November

1910. They settled in what was later called Dollins Canyon just north west of Curtis Canyon.

It was presumed that Nora met him as a neighbor and they started dating. Nora dated him for seven years before getting married.

She waited until Andrew was old enough to accept him, he must have been about twelve years old when they married. She may also have been waiting until Melvin proved himself to be trustworthy.

Aunt Nora was a small woman weighing (maybe) 100 lbs. soaking wet. But she was able to discipline the big strapping boys and had that reputation.

She was quite a horsewoman and kept chickens. She would keep one separate and feed it gruel for a time before slaughter. She cooked her salsa all day on the stove and they had beans at least once a week.

She and her sister Rosie were very close and must have lived fairly close. When Rosie would visit Nora, sometimes she would wring the chicken's necks for her.

Rosie married Bob Greer, and I think he was quite a bit older than she. They had a set of twins (a boy and a girl) but they died at birth. Bob and Rosie owned and ran a hardware store in Bayrd, New Mexico until Bob passed away and then Rosie ran it, until her health got bad. I remember Aunt Rosie as my dad and family would drive over to see her once in awhile. They lived in the back of the store and I loved to go there and look around in the store at all the stuff they had in it.

When she passed away we went to her funeral. I was very young but it really made me sad as I had grown to love her.

One time Nora, Rosie and Gail (Nora's daughter) went to the cemetery to visit Bob's grave and Rosie fell down on his grave and cried.

Nora had E.S.P. qualities, and shocked the family a few times with her intuitions. Andrew would take off for long periods of time for various work and travel. One day when he had been gone for months, Nora announced, "Andrew is coming home today." She cleaned the house from top to bottom very happily, cooked a grand meal, dressed up her table for guests and then Gail heard a motorcycle coming. She ran out the door excitedly to see Andrew coming and ran directly off the porch

Rosa V. Curtis, last child born to Joel W. and Rosalina Curtis

into the air. Andrew picked her up off the ground and took her in the house.

There was another time when Nora and Gail were at a church revival meeting in the evening. In the middle of the service Nora punched Gail and said, "We've got to go home, Vivan is sick". Gail said "Let's wait til' the service is over." Nora told her "I'm going with or without you!" So they left. When they arrived home Vivan was in convulsions, which had come upon her suddenly. Nora knew how to take care of Vivan and Gail made the statement "Mother is a pretty good doctor." She educated Vivan at home.

Norah 'Nora' O. Jane Curtis, Joel Warner Curtis,
Antonio 'Tony' Malush Curtis

(1896) Joel was blind in the photo.

One weekend when Gail was home from doing graduate studies in Albuquerque, N.M.., The phone rang and Nora began screaming "Andrew, Andrew!" The call was to inform them that Andrew had been run over by a train while trying to get on, and was killed. Melvin went to identify the body, and he told Gail that his hair was dyed red from the blood. He was a handsome blond, and the ladies loved him. Gail left school for six weeks to take care of Nora and then returned and completed her semester.

Andrew was married when he died but the family lost track of his widow.

Vivan had a lot of trouble through her life and Nora said as a toddler, she had fallen and hit her head against the stove, and that all her troubles were caused by that. I was told, when I was a small child, and saw Vivan in her wheel chair, that she had polio and that was the reason she couldn't walk any more, but I found out that was not true.

Gail's daughter stated "We'll never know the answer to this, but Nora massaged Vivan's legs daily and put her through physical regiments daily.

Gail said "I think it is a great testimony to mother and her care for Vivan that she lived to be seventy two."

Nora had breast cancer at the age of sixty or so. They went to Missouri, for her cancer treatment, which was a mastectomy and some kind of chemical burn. Her incision never healed completely because she continued to lift Vivan. She died in her sixties with liver cancer, which must have been very similar to the way Vivan died.

Nora and Melvin had two daughters: Gail Curtis Dollins, born January 30, 1917, at Mayhill, N.M. She married Robert Vaughn Brashears on October 20, 1944 at the First Baptist Church, Las Cruces, N.M. His birth date was July 7, 1915 in Monroe County, Missouri.

Gail and Robert 'Bob' had three children: Melvin Richard was born November 11, 1945 in Alamogordo, N.M. and he married Victoria Lynn Fuqua on June 9, 1966 in Green Chapel, University of MO, Columbia, MO. She was born November 27, 1946 in Hannibal, MO. The second child was Donald Robert and he was born May 23, 1947 in Mexico, MO and he married Deborah Jane Williams on December 20, 1969 in Newmann Center, Columbia, MO. She was born December 4, 1948 in Granite City, IL. The third child was Patricia Gail and she was born March 18, 1950, in Hannibal, MO. She married John Robert Grimmett, on December 30, 1979 at Perry Baptist. John was born on September 1951 in Berkeley, California.

Nora's and Melvin's other child was Vivan Lisbon Dollins. She was in a wheel chair all of her life and never married.

Gail passed away on October 3, 1986 and Vivan passed away a few years back and was buried in the Alamogordo cemetery .

During the late 1800's and early 1900's a lot of other pioneer families were coming to the area to settle.

They came from the states of Texas, Missouri, Tennessee, and other mid' and eastern states, a westward bound people with a better life in their hearts and minds.

Of two such families were the Jernigans and Carrs.

George Jernigan was born in 1850 and Dizzy M. Carr was born on March 4, 1849. They were married on Jan 10, 1876 and left Texas in May of 1891 traveling with the Carr family. Mr. Wiley Carr was her father.

The Carrs settled on land on the Upper Peñasco, for awhile, near the Curtis place, and the Jernigans homesteaded on one hundred and sixty acres near Weed, New Mexico on Perk Canyon.

In 1896 and 1898 they purchased two other places. The last one they moved to, in 1899, and it became known as the Jernigan Ranch. This ranch was west of Duncan and East of Weed.

George and Dizzy had seven children but one died at birth. Listed in order were Wiley born November 22, 1844, Robert Henry born January 5, 1880, Ernest Edward called "Buckskin" born September 5, 1882, Curtis Lee called "Dee" born June 19, 1884, Ida Evelyn born March 15, 1886, and Dizzy M. that was born on February 20, 1888.

They became very well known, as most of the settlers did, and Wiley at one time became a very wealthy cattleman, rancher, and land owner.

One time, when my sister Louise was talking to my Grandmother Maggie, she told Lou she had been engaged to be married to another man, other than Tony. Then a few years back while visiting with a cousin she told me that her mother had told her that Grandma had been engaged to marry a Jernigan. I found out that it was Dee Jernigan. No other details were ever given except that there was a discrepancy in their religious faith preference and Maggie's parents disapproved, so she broke it off and married Tony Curtis on January 7, 1903 by a Baptist minister, Milton Raeca and their witnesses were W.D. McDorman and W.R. Potter. The marriage took place at Fred and Sarah Brantley's home.

Dee married Ethel Watts but their marriage did not last and he married Nellie Watts.

In the 1920's there was a horrible drought in the mountains and Dee bought a ranch near Deming, New Mexico.

The Watts family was connected to the Joy family as was the Cadys, and Van Winkles. Ed Watts married Dizzy Jernigan and there was a story told by Will Parker about a horse race between Ed Watts and Charley Van Winkle. They usually ran their races for a pound of candy, but this day they matched it for two weeks later, for five dollars, on a run of one hundred and fifty yards. Because that was too far for the short town roadway, they made a deal with Dan Stephens to run the race in his field. After the two weeks were up, and from getting their horses in shape, a big crowd gathered that day to watch. Ed had ridden several races but Charley was inexperienced and Ed won the race. Someone made the comment "watch that boy ride, like a bat out of hell".

The first store built in Mayhill by F.C. Hunter photo from 1909

This was just some of the sport and entertainment of that day.

By the late 1800's the New Mexico Territories were flourishing with new people from all over the, now existing, United States and Mayhill was one of these places, as it had a well tolerated climate with good growing seasons.

In 1897 Charles Eddy started construction on the railroad from El Paso, Texas and in January of 1898 it crossed the New Mexico line. Otero County was created from parts of Dona Ana and Lincoln Counties in 1899 and as part of the enticement to become a new County, it was named for the governor at that time, Miguel Otero.

I can see why these people chose to settle here and not just because it was good land but also because of it's beauty. I remember the mountains that I grew up in, and how nice it was in the summers. It was cool compared to some of the more desert like land surrounding it. It had a vast wilderness of pinon, pine, and oak. It also had aspen in the higher parts and what my folks called oak shinnery, that were oak bushes growing throughout the trees and in the fall they were so beautiful in reds, oranges, and yellows. There were creeks and springs all over, and I remember one spring that we used to go to for picnics . It was in Curtis Canyon and was called The Goat Camp Springs.

In the evenings you could sit out on the porch and hear the wind rustling through the trees, and doves cooing in the distance, and the owls making their hooting sounds. We loved to watch the fire flies and sometimes try to catch them. The families all became close and neighbor helped neighbor and they intermarried, so that you were usually kin to most everyone.

Near Weed, New Mexico there was a small place known as Wright, NM and in 1901 a family, by the name of Allen, came from Texas and homesteaded here. The home was built in Keen Canyon, about five miles from Weed, but was later renamed Allen Canyon.

The Allens had a daughter named Edith Perrene Allen that was three years old when they moved here. She was born on March 5, 1898 in Crosby county, Texas. Cloudcroft at this time was booming with tourist and a coach brought some of these folks to the Allen place and Mrs. Allen would board them. This would be vacations for the tourist. She served them meals and some would stay a few days, others weeks at a time. Mr. D.P. Allen ran the Wright Post Office and a country store. When Edith was fourteen on Jan 6, 1912 her mother told her and her siblings that New Mexico had become a State.

Edith married Monroe David Brantley, son of Fred Brantley, on April 12, 1915, at the Allen family home. Their wedding trip was by horse and buggy through Weed and Mayhill to the Forest Service lookout tower where Monroe was a fire lookout.

In 1917 they purchased the General Mercantile store in Mayhill from J.E.C. Bell and Charles Bell. Monroe was appointed Postmaster and a section of the store was made into a Post Office. The original structure built by F.C. Hunter was of wood, in the early 1930's the wooden building was torn down and replaced with the now existing building of river rock. The rock ranging in size from grapefruit to bowling ball size was hauled by horse and wagon and trucks. It was built during the Depression and help for building came from folks in the community. The rock mason was John Wake and the finish carpenter was Will Buckner.

Mayhill store, hotel, cafe, and service station somewhere around 1930's or 40's, built by Monroe and Edith Brantley

Monroe and Edith had three daughters, Hattie Perrene born at Mayhill on February 24, 1916, Flora Hazel born January 8, 1919 at Mayhill, and Lylah Lois "Billye" born March 27, 1927 at Mayhill. Billye told me, "My name, Lylah, came from a dear friend of my family who lived in El Paso, Texas. She had six boys and my mom had three girls. I became her namesake. I loved the lady and even lived with her family and finished high school in El Paso, but I never related to the name. She was such a dear, she didn't even try to make me feel bad about it." So this explains how she came to be called Billye.

Monroe was Post Master in Mayhill for twenty seven years and they decided to sell. During the years in Mayhill they added a café, Hotel and service station to the already existing grocery business. They sold out in 1944 and bought a ranch at Hope, New Mexico. They were there a few years and moved to Artesia, New Mexico due to the failing health of Monroe. He passed away on October 18, 1953 and Edith traded their Artesia property for the Camino Court in Carlsbad, New Mexico because Carlsbad is where Perrene and her family were living. Edith operated the court for quite a few years and then went into the Lakeview "Christian home that was established by the churches of Christ. She was honored in Cloudcroft in 1985 as one of the pioneers and passed away on March 4, 1991.

Perrene married Henry Roy Kemper In Mayhill, New Mexico on June 2, 1935. He was born in Melrose, New Mexico on March 3, 1910. They had two children: R.H. 'Red' Jr. born March 28, 1939 in El Paso, Texas. Red passed away on April 20, 2008 from a long illness. Their second child was Patricia Ann 'Pati', and she was born on September 16, 1948 in Carlsbad, New Mexico.

I remember playing with Red when I was little and it seems really funny to me now to think back on it. He was called Red because he had the most beautiful red hair you ever saw and freckles.

When I was born, having Cherokee Indian blood from my mothers side, I was very dark with a shock of cole black hair and very dark skinned. My eyes were so black that you could not distinguish the pupils of my eyes from the rest. Uncle Monroe and Aunt Edith came to see me and when Uncle Monroe picked me up he said "Well hello little Blackie" and that is what that family called me all my life. So when my folks were ready to go, after our visits, they would come out and call "Red, Blackie it's time to come in."

Hazel married Oliver James Underwood on November 25, 1937 in Mayhill, New Mexico. They had four children: Larry Oliver born July 21, 1938 in Roswell, New Mexico; Lynda Jo born June 6, 1940 in Hotel

Diex, El Paso, Texas and died In Clovis, New Mexico as a small child; James Karen born September 21, 1944 in El Paso, Texas; Billy Lynn born December 26, 1949 in Deming, New Mexico.

Lylah Lois 'Billye' married Herbert H. Renwick born December 23, 1928 in Sycamore, Illinios on August 12, 1950. Their wedding was a garden wedding at her home in Hope, New Mexico. They had a Bar BQ, and reception there after the wedding.

I remember the wedding, I was ten years old and at a very impressionable age. I thought Billye was one of the most beautiful women I had ever seen. She was always special to me after that.

Billye and Herbert had two children: Debra Ann born March 26, 1953 at the Roswell, New Mexico Air Force Base; Herbert H. Renwick Jr. born March 21, 1957 in Elgin, Illinois. Herbert Jr. married Debra Lee Crowley in Rolling Meadows, Illinois on December 23, 1989 and they have two children: Chase Harley born June 29, 1994 in Elgin, Illinois, and Megan Blake born May 14, 1999 in Elgin, Illinois.

Monroe was the brother of Maggie Curtis and previous to her Marriage, her sister Alice "Allie" married William Clark in September of 1898 and they had 7 children. Monroe Hobson born October 6, 1899 and died December 28, 1971, Ethel Elizabeth born January 4, 1902 and died May 7, 1976, Lewis Fredric born February 23, 1906, Edith Pearl born August 4, 1911 and died 1958, William Jack born October 16, 1914 and died October 7, 1917, Pauline Alma born December 15, 1917, Sarah Eliza born November 20, 1921 and died November 7, 1945. The family moved to Califronia and spent their lives there. I have no knowledge of Allie's death or where she is buried but William is buried at Tulare Cemetery, Tulare, California.

The Lathams had settled in the Burnt Canyon area. There were several children in the family and two girls, Ethel and Mae, married two of the Brantley boys, Lee and Mark.

Ethel was born on February 17, 1899 but her birthplace is unknown. The family moved to the area when Ethel was a small child. Lee met Ethel and married her on April 8, 1917. He was a cowhand most of his life, working for various privately owned ranches. The Diamond A and the Flying H being two of them.

Lee became executor of the Fredric Brantley estate in the late 1940's. He then started running the 7B, as the ranch was called, for several years.

He sold it to Curley Derrick in the early 50's and he and Ethel moved to Mayhill where he built and operated a Phillips 66 service station for about fifteen years.

Lee had just been married a short time when Will Parker asked if he would like to go and farm for him on the Felix. It sounded good to Lee and Ethel both, to have the job, so they took it.

Will and his wife then moved in the old Headwater Ranch house where a Frenchman, by the name of John Tunstall, lived when the Lincoln County War started. Billy the Kid was working for Mr. Tunstall at that time. Will's first life as a cowboy was on this old Tunstall Ranch, which was called the Flying H Ranch in Wills time. He began working on the ranch in the early 1900's and what he knew about the old Lincoln County War days he learned from the old time cowboys he worked with.

The story they told was: "At the beginning of the War, early one morning of the day that Mr. Tunstall was killed, he and Billy the Kid left the Headwater Ranch on the Felix River, on their way to Lincoln."

In those days there was an old wagon road that went up Lincoln Canyon, close to the Apache Indian Reservation. This old road went through what has always been called the Lake country. This old wagon road went through several of these lakes. The first lake was called Burro Lake, then Deep Lake, then Flying H Lake, and then last Diamond Lake.

Just after this old road passed Diamond Lake, it crossed Casey Canyon. It was named for the Caseys because they lived on the Hondo where Casey Canyon ran into the Hondo, just above Picacho.

When Mr. Tunstall and Billy the Kid crossed Casey Canyon to the north side, Tunstall met his death. Billy the Kid, saw the men coming toward them, and saved his life by hiding a ways away from Tunstall.

When the mob met Tunstall they killed him and his horse.

The mob left and headed back to Lincoln, and Billy went where Tunstall and his horse had been killed. He then told himself, "I will live to kill every one of them blood thirsty coyotes," and according to history, he did. Will learned a lot of history from an old Indian Chief also, when he was working for the Indian government, along with all the stories told by the old cowboys.

Sometime around 1962, Lee sold the station and went into retirement. He was a very tall and slender built man with a heart of gold.

The men throughout the area would gather at his station and visit, telling their tales of the times. They lived in a big two story house on 'The Lane', that went to the school house and the church of Christ building.

There was a trait of sorts in the family and Lee possessed it, among others in the family, including my father, Veolan Curtis, and myself. We had a tendency for nightmares and sleepwalking. Ethel had a baby girl, and as usual during those days, most of the babys born were born in their homes. One night when the baby was a few days old Lee had a nightmare and jumped up and turned the bed upside down on Ethel and the baby. They were not hurt but very much startled. Lee told them the next day "I was dreaming of yesterday when Cara and I were bailing hay. I dreamed that the tractor had turned over on Cara and I was trying to get him out from under it."

Another time he was hunting with some of the men and they had a tent set up out in the forest. Lee dreamed that a bear was in the tent and jumped up and ran a way down the hill barefoot and in his long johns before he woke up and realized it was a dream. He could hardly walk all the next day because of his sore feet.

Lee and Ethel had three children, Clara Lee that married Willie Stirman and they had a girl named Mary Beth. Mary Beth was one of my sister's best friends and in the same class at school. They were the only ones to graduate eighth grade from the Mayhill school in 1950. Clara died when Mary Beth was a very young child and Willie (or Bill as I knew him) finished raising her. Bill ran the Mayhill Café for several years and he and Mary Beth lived behind the hotel lobby, where the stairs were, in two small rooms.

I heard a story about Bill when I was very young that he and Clara were visiting Grandpa Fred and Grandma Sarah one day and a storm came up. Bill walked out on the front porch to see what it was like and a bolt of lightning hit a post on the porch and it ricochet off onto his head. It traveled down his back and one of his legs. Someone there, I'm not sure who, ran out and was able to revive him but it was said that he had a scar that ran from the back of his head all the way down one leg into the bottom of his foot. I saw the scar on the back of his head and he never did have hair to grow there. He was crippled in that leg and used a cane all his life.

The second child born to Lee and Ethel was Arvel Lincoln. I remember Arvel but not real well. He left the mountains and found work elsewhere. When my family moved back to the mountains in 1958 he was back home in poor health, he was known to have a drinking problem. The third child was Mary Belle. Mary married William Travis Harrell and they had two sons: Dennis Edward Harrell born September 11, 1941 and William 'Billy' Wayne Harrell born March 11, 1944.

William and Mary divorced when Billy Wayne was a small baby and he and Dennis was taken in by Lee and Ethel and they raised them.

Mark as I mentioned before, along with his brother Lee, married a Latham girl, Ethel's sister. Her name was Mary May and they married on November 14, 1912 in Mayhill. They had three children. Reba Lillian was born May 13, 1914. Alva Owen was born March 16, 1919, and Preston Shelby was born October 2, 1928.

Reba married Ivan Andrews and they had two children, a boy and a girl. Alva married Eileen and they had three children, a boy and two girls. Preston married Jeanne Sheppard and they had three children, Twin boys, Gerald and Darrell and one girl Judy.

Mary 'Mamie' Lue Brantley met William 'Willie' Hardwin Frizzell one summer when she decided to further her education during summer school. The school was on James Canyon at the Pine Springs schoolhouse. They married on December 24, 1914 at the Brantley home.

Willie was born September 13, 1890 in Burnet County, Texas, the youngest of three children of John Talbert and Margaret Serepta 'Baird' Frizzell. Bushwhackers reportedly killed John Talbert in 1892 in Marshall, Harrison County, Texas as he and his family were traveling from Texas to the Territory of New Mexico.

Margaret's family had settled at Pine Springs on James Canyon in the 1880's. Sometime after the death of John Talbert, Margaret's brother Tate Baird traveled to Texas and brought his sister and her two youngest sons, Robert and Willie to New Mexico. John Wesley, the oldest son remained in Texas.

It is unknown where the family lived after arriving at the home of Tate. Perhaps they lived with his family or on his homestead. The boys apparently helped him on the farm. Robert eventually went back to Texas. Margaret became ill and was taken to the Indian Agency, for medical attention, where she died in 1920. She is buried in the James Canyon Cemetery.

The first home of the newly weds was on James Canyon on the Homestead of The Bairds. Willie was farming for his Uncle Tate. In 1915, their first child, Eva Noriene was born on October 15th . They had lived and worked there for about two years when they had the opportunity to buy a claim in Burnt Canyon from Earl and Lizzie Paxton. They lived on the claim off and on until they proved up on it in 1920. During these years, two more daughters were added to the family: Ara Irue was born in 1918 and Thelma Ellie November 20,1919.

For a short time they moved back to James Canyon and farmed for Emit Gregg. In the fall of 1920 they had the opportunity to go to work for Robert McGee whose farm was only a short distance from Mamie's parents on the Peñasco river. Mr. McGee had homesteaded one hundred and sixty acres in 1880. Now that he was an elderly man, he wanted a family to live with him to farm and tend the house. They felt very fortunate to get this job. Mr. McGee had a good farm and orchard, and since they would be working for a share of the crops, this was a good opportunity.

In December of 1922, Mamie and Little Ara took Typhoid Fever. Ara died on January 27, 1923. After her death, Mamie had a relapse and for about thirty days, those caring for her thought each day would be her last. But she survived the terrible ordeal. Her health improved and she was soon back to caring for her family. She cooked for the farm hands, and was helping get the crops, especially the apples, to market.

The next year, in 1924, their only son, William Aris was born and in 1925 Lora Lue was born.

Everyone was healthy and happy, and crops were good. In September 1928, Willie suddenly became ill and was taken to Alamogordo for medical attention. He was diagnosed with Nephritis and died a few days later. This was a terrible shock for Mamie and her young family. She was sure Mr. McGee would want to hire another family to farm for him, and undoubtedly wondered how she would provide for her family.

Mr. McGee was now seventy eight years old. Having no family of his own, he loved the Frizzell's as though they were his own. He begged Mamie to stay with him and care for him until his death. In return he would deed the farm to her. They remained with him, hiring local men to farm and do the chores that Mamie and the kids were not able to do.

He died in 1933 at the age of eighty three. Mamie buried him in James Canyon Cemetery near the grave of her husband.

Mamie continued to live on the farm until 1935 when her brother Lee took over the farm and she moved her family further up the Peñasco to Graveyard Canyon. In 1942 she moved back to the McGee farm and John L. Parker farmed it for her. In 1943 Mamie sold it as well as the homestead in Burnt Canyon to John L. And Leah 'Posey' Parker. The Parkers owned the farm at the Headwater Spring. Mamie moved into their house and they moved to the McGee place. She later moved to Mayhill where she lived until moving to Carlsbad, New Mexico in 1950.

She was a kind, gentle, woman who portrayed a remarkable strength as a mother and business woman during an era and in a profession that was considered a man's world. She was loved and respected by her family, friends and neighbors, and was a faithful member of the church of Christ. She was a wonderful Christian influence on many. Lora, Mamie's youngest daughter, told "Mother took care of Sarah, her mother, in her home in Mayhill until Sarah's death on August 24, 1946

Mamie died in 1986 and was buried in the James Canyon cemetery next to her husband and Mr. McGee, and many of the connected families already buried there.

Eva, the oldest child of Mamie and Willie, after his death, assumed the role of going to school, doing chores such as feeding the hogs and helping care for her younger brother and sisters. Eva knew and accepted the fact that she had a lot of responsibility.

There was family by the name of Grice that were members of the local church of Christ in Mayhill as were the Frizzell's so it was inevitable that Eva should meet Jack.

Jack DeEdison Grice was the oldest of five children born on September 4, 1915 in Cleveland, Tennessee to Will and Ruby 'Watkins' Grice. Will, Ruby and family moved from Tennessee to Mayhill in 1932 where they began farming on Cox Canyon.

The grade school children went to school in Mayhill in a small two room school house but the high school students (the ninth through the twelfth grades) were bused to Cloudcroft. Jack and Eva both recalled some of the scary rides.

Several times the boys had to push the bus through the heavy snow to get to school. One time John Pendergrass, a young man about six feet tall, stepped off the bus to help push, and stepped into snow up to his waist. They had to push the bus to the school parking lot in order to turn around and had to wait two to three hours before they could return home.

Since both the Grice family and the Frizzell family went to church together Jack and Eva started dating, different families in the area would have parties on Saturday, a lot of these parties were on Miller Flats and everyone would ride their horses. The songs Jack remembered most are Little Brown Jug and Shoo Fly.

Jack and Eva were married December 1, 1934 in Roswell, New Mexico by a preacher named Mr. Jeffcoat. The ceremony took place in Mr. and Mrs. Jeffcoat's house with Jack's parents and Eva's mother witnessing the ceremony. There was too much work to do at home so their trip back to Mayhill was their honeymoon. After they married they lived in a small house that had been built on the 7B Ranch, near Fred's and Sarah's house and they worked for Fred.

On October 22, 1942 while still living at the 7B, Velma Ann was born in Sacramento at Dr. Shield's house. Eva had gone to stay with the Dr. and his wife, awaiting the birth of her first baby. Doctor Shields was the Doctor for the railroad.

Jack joined the Army on September 19, 1944, signing his enlistment papers at the Baird's place on James Canyon. He was inducted into duty at Ft. Bliss, Texas. He was sent to Camp Hood, Texas; Ft. Ord, CA; Vancouver, WA; boarded ship in Oregon; Island of Ohau, HA; Saipan; Okinawa; Mendora Philippines; Manila; Back to the States in San Francisco, CA. He was discharged as Sgt. (Squad Leader) at Ft. Bliss, Texas, January 20, 1946. While serving in the Asiatic Pacific Theater Jack received the Asiatic Pacific theater Ribbon, Philippine Liberation Ribbon, Good Conduct Medal, Purple Heart, Bronze Star with Oak Leaf Clusters, and the Victory Medal.

During Jack's time in the service Eva and Velma stayed in Mayhill. In 1947 Jack and Eva were expecting another baby. Ross Hooten took Jack, Eva and Velma to Hobbs in Mr. Hooten's father's car. They were going to stay with Jack's parents who had moved there. Thyria Lue was born on October 1, 1947. The family of four returned to Mayhill, however, Thyria did not tolerate the altitude of over six thousand feet, and had trouble breathing, so Jack found work in Carlsbad at Young Implement Company. He was working with Hubert Cope, who had also lived in Mayhill, and was well known by the family. Hubert was married to Lena Marie 'Potter', the sister of Kenneth Potter Jr.

Mamie had bought a home in Carlsbad, when she moved there in 1950, at 1508 West Fox Street. She asked Jack and Eva to move in with her, and they did. Eva took very good care of her mother. Eva made many trips to Roswell to be with Mamie when she had to be hospitalized. They eventually moved into their own home.

In 1951 Eva was expecting another baby. Sarah Willene was born on December 18, 1951 in Carlsbad, and in 1952 Jack took a job with the City of Hobbs which lasted two and a half years. They then moved back to Carlsbad. Jack worked at a variety of jobs in different places for some time.

Eva chose to stay home with her three daughters and was very active in all of their activities. She was a life member of the PTA. As the girls got older she took in ironing in order for them to have extra spending money. The girls have memories of their mother standing at the ironing board with terrific headaches, but would not let them slow her down. Eva was a very hard worker, and had such a tender heart. She managed motels near their home so that the owners could have a break. She cleaned houses for several ladies with whom she had become friends. While Jack was working in the ranching field, Eva was cooking for the roundups. She really enjoyed that. There may not have been much in the cupboard but she was able to prepare a feast out of nothing.

Eva was a sweet and wonderful woman and well liked by everyone. She loved her children and grandchildren immensely.

I remeber one time, when my mother and I were visiting with Eva. She had one of the grandchildren there and they were making cookies. The little girl had a foot stool and was standing on it by Eva so she could reach the cupboard to help. Eva was so patient with her and they acted like it was a game.

I heard a story from some of the family, about when Eva and Jack were living on the Brantley Ranch, that she was taking Grandpa Fred to the doctor in Roswell. The roads, for quit a few miles, were still dirt roads and pretty rough. He was fussing about the rough roads but when they got on the paved roads he told her "Ok, Eva, you can take the bridle off."

My dad and Eva were close to the same age and he told me that they played together a lot when they were growing up and then double dated when they got older. Jack and dad got along famously, and after they were both married, they were together a lot, rabbit hunting or on picnics together.

Jack had a motorcycle, at one time, and they were down on the flats toward Artesia rabbit hunting and dad got on the motorcycle with Jack and they were riding out across the prairie when they hit a Prairie Dog hole and they both went flying and dad ended up in a cactus. My mother spent all afternoon getting the cactus spine out of him.

Velma Ann married Robert Leighton Brown on February 15, 1962 and they live in Carlsbad. They have two daughters that also live in Carlsbad.

Kellie married Wayne Brown and has two daughters, Dannett and Lacey. Becky married Johnny Waldrop and has two sons Justin and Lane.

Thyria Lue married William DeWayne Canada on January 4, 1966. They also lived in Carlsbad. DeWayne passed away May 19, 1996. They had a son and a daughter, Tracy and his wife Wyetta, also live in Carlsbad and have three children, Dyar, Ashley and Tori. Kim and her husband John Yarc live in Phoenix, AZ. Thyria married Jay Loftis on November 10, 2001 and they live in Carlsbad.

Sarah Willene married Norman Miles on March 19, 1971 and they live in Lovington, New Mexico. They have two daughters, Mandi and her husband Ernie Wheeler that live in Hobbs and they have four children, Allie, Sydni, Lynsey and Cutter. Kristin lives in Amarillo, Texas.

Eva passed away on March 1, 2001 and Jack passed away September 17, 2003.

Thelma Ellie met and married Jessie Raymond Samford. His parents were Alva Charles and Greta Jewel 'Blankenship' Samford. His parents, he and his siblings were born in Texas. During a few travels else where they ended up on the Peñasco River and worked at a sawmill just below Mayhill in the summer of 1935.

The Samfords and the Frizzells were both members of the church of Christ and this seems to be a story retold but Raymond and Thelma met at church. They went to a Christmas party at Hazel Brantley's and got to know each other better there. They were married in Alamogordo, New Mexico on February 26, 1936.

Mamie gave Thelma five dollars and she bought a dress and a pair of shoes with it for her wedding.

Their first home was the little house on the Brantley place that Jack and Eva had lived in. Raymond worked at the sawmill for awhile then they moved to Artesia and he worked for a Mr. Campbell on a cotton farm. He worked there a year and a W.P.A. road job came open on Cox Canyon and they bought a tent and moved up where the job was, and he worked there for awhile.

Raymond didn't have a car so they caught rides on the mail car when they needed to go to town. Thelma made the statement "Here we ate tree squirrels."

Their next move was to Mamie's place that she eventually sold to John L. Parker. While there, their apples froze during a hard spring, and the wheat crop was washed away during heavy rains. Because of this they had to pay their grocery bill with the profit from the calf sales.

Raymond and Thelma had four girls: first was Wanda Virginia born December 19, 1938, she married Willliam 'Bill' Stanley Stanbrough. He was born May 11, 1936. They had three children; Wanetta, Dwain 'Tiger', and Johnny. Second was Patsy Marie born July 3, 1940, she married Fred Carol Griffin. He was born November 27, 1939. They had Three girls; Kathy, Carol and Norma. Third was Carolin Joyce born October 12, 1941. She married Leonard Wayne Scott and they had three children; the first baby died, Wayne, and Yvonne. Fourth was Shirley Adelia born January 11, 1946 at Tony and Maggie's place and she was named Adelia after Maggie. She married James Thomas Summers and they had three children; Kevin, Kendal, and Kimberly.

Raymond was an avid hunter. He always had a deer come hunting season. He taught Thelma and the girls how to hunt and Thelma and Virginia made good hunters but the other girls didn't like it as well. Virginia loved to hunt with her dad and went as much as possible. After she married Bill he would go along and vowed to be as good a hunter as Raymond.

Raymond worked several jobs, one was at Timberon and then was hired for the County as a blade man. He was a foreman for the State Highway Dept. and worked seven years for Jimmy Mayhill on the ZA Ranch.

Kenneth Jr. and Lena Marie Potter became close friends with them and while they had no car the Potters would stop and get them for worship services, and for parties that were thrown, quite a bit, during those days.

Kenneth Potter Jr. married Lanell Dockray, the daughter of Cleve and Cressie 'Arthur' Dockray. There were three other children born to Cleve and Cressie; Glenn that married a Mr. Tunnell (he was a school teacher at Mayhill), and Mable that married Ross Hooten, and a son named David that died when he was very young.

My dad and mother were very close friends with Ross and Mable and my dad told me about David being one of his best friends when they were young. I don't know for sure how old he was or what happened that he died but I know it made an impact on dad's life.

Some time later Raymond and Thelma bought an acre of land from Mamie and built a three room house. This was where Marie and Carolin were born. Sometime around 1947 they bought a house from Grandpa and Grandma Samford in Mayhill. It was across the street from where Mamie eventually bought.

I remember one specific time going to stay the night with Marie, which I did a lot, and we went to grandma Samford's house. She got out the story book of Snow White and let us dress up and act out some of the story as she read to us. All the children called all the older women of the community grandma.

There was Grandma Samford, Grandma Stirman, Grandma Curtis, etc. They were all like my grandmas, and they all were good Christian guides for us children with discipline and lots of love for us all.

My folks spent a lot of time with Raymond and Thelma and one time that I remember was when Raymond had taken an old car and cut the top off and put wooden benches all around in the back and made a rabbit hunting 'Jalopie'. Raymond and Dad got in the front seat with Mother and Thelma between them and all of us kids piled in the back and down the road we went. They drove down to the flat country past the Flying H Ranch and took off out into the flats and when they found a rabbit or rabbits they would stop and shoot them until they thought they had enough for supper. We kids laughed and jumped up and down and had a ball on that trip. After we got back to their house they cleaned the rabbits and Thelma and Mother cooked them. We had a delicious supper and a lot of fun that day.

Thelma was a hard worker and I remember seeing her iron a big basket full of clothes. She ironed everything, even the socks and under clothes. She also canned the deer meat that they killed and always set a good meal on the table.

Raymond passed away on March 12, 1987. Thelma lived in their home at Mayhill until she couldn't take care of herself anymore, and went to live in the Betty Dare Nursing Home in Alamogordo. She passed away on August 1, 1988. They are both buried at Mayhill.

William Aris married Juanice Parker on May 15, 1943 in High Rolls, New Mexico. The train track ran near the minister's house, but they did not expect a train and parked the car on the train track. During the ceremony, Aris had to run out to move the car! Witnesses to the marriage were the young couple's parents, maternal grandparents and cousins Billye Brantley and Eleanor Posey.

Juanice Parker was born August 9, 1925 at the home of her grandparents, Johnny and Lizzie Posey. Their home was located about three miles west of Mayhill on James Canyon. Juanice was the only child born to John L. and Leah Posey Parker. At the time of her birth, John L. and Leah were living at the Frizzell place in Graveyard Canyon. Several of her childhood years were spent living at Elk, New Mexico where her father farmed for Angie Cleve. She started to school at Elk and moved to Mayhill in 1936. She graduated from Cloudcroft High School in 1943.

Aris and his sister Thelma were especially close as she was the one who helped him with the outdoor chores while the other girls helped mostly in the house. They loved to pull pranks on each other, and enjoyed laughing about those pranks as adults!

Aris attended school in Mayhill through the eighth grade then high school in Cloudcroft where he graduated in 1942. He had high regard for several of his teachers, particularly Mr. Haile and Mr. Tunnell. He participated in sports where he was on the football and basketball teams.

The newly weds made their first home on the farm in Graveyard Canyon. Aris truck farmed, did day work for other farmers, worked on road jobs, etc. In 1944 their first child, Hilda was born at their home. Cressie Dockray and Onie Clayton attended the birth on a very snowy night!

World War II was in full swing and the young men from the community were going to war. Some were enlisting and some were being drafted. In February, 1945 Aris enlisted in the U.S. Navy and was soon off to boot camp in San Diego, California. On August 3, he boarded the ship LST 482 and they set sail for the South Pacific. His job aboard ship included swab jockey, mess cook, and assistant cook. He was fortunate to not be included in any conflicts. The war ended with the surrender of Japan in September 1945 and Aris was discharged April 5, 1946.

After the war, Aris, Juanice and Hilda settled down once again to "life on the farm". In 1952 a son, Gerald William was born in Roswell, New Mexico. That same year, Aris went to work for Potash Company of America in Carlsbad, New Mexico and moved his family to town. They continued to live there until 1959. The saying is true that contends that you can take the boy out of the country, but you can't take the country out of the boy! In May 1959 they returned to Mayhill. He built a house on the John L. Parker home place and went to work for the U.S. Forest Service.

In March 1960, another daughter, Teresa was born in Carlsbad, New Mexico.

Aris continued to work for the Forest Service in Timber Management until his retirement in 1989. He administered timber sales, thinning projects, wood sales and was a certified timber scaler. He was a member of the Mayhill Fire Department and served a term as Fire Chief. During this time, Juanice cared for the family home and worked part time for the U.S. Forest Service as Sacramento District Clerk and later as a sales clerk for Mayhill Mercantile.

All three of their children graduated from Cloudcroft High School.

Hilda has remained in the Mayhill area and works for Peñasco Valley Telephone Cooperative. Gerald graduated from New Mexico Military Institute and then enlisted in the U.S. Navy where he made a career as a Hospital Corpsman. He is retired and lives in Jacksonville, North Carolina. Teresa graduated from New Mexico State University with an associate degree in Nursing. She is an RN and works in Obstetrics in Victoria, Texas. Aris and Juanice have seven living grandsons and two great granddaughters. Two grandsons died in infancy.

Aris and Juanice continued to live on the McGee homestead where Aris was born. He enjoyed having a few cows and raising a garden. Juanice was a member of the Mayhill Extension Club and a member of the board of directors for the Mayhill Community Building. Both of them, were always, very community minded and willing to go the extra mile for a project that would benefit Mayhill.

Juanice passed away a few years ago and Aris lives in an assisted living home in Alamogordo, New Mexico.

Lora married Kenneth W. Thomason. He was born on July 29, 1926, the son of Clay B. and Josephine 'Josie' K. Thomason, that bought the grocery store from Bill Stirman.

Lora wrote "Growing up in Mayhill, New Mexico was like one big family, every one working hard to just make a living, but we had a lot of good times as well. Church was a big part of our lives. Aris and I took turns riding to church with Grandma and Grandpa, Fred and Sarah Brantley, in the wagon."

Lora was nine months old when her father, Willie Frizzell, died. She knows how hard it was on her mother, Mamie, and remembers the harvest times, neighbors and relatives were always there to help. Everyone would go from place to place; even at hog killing time, to help each other out.

Mamie was really good about trying to keep them happy as well as busy. On bad, stormy days they would 'bundleup', go to the barn and shuck corn. They would sing, mostly church hymns, with Thelma leading, while they worked. Time went faster and they would get a lot of corn done, which saved time when feeding. They all had every day chores to do.

They had a nice gentle horse, 'Old Bonnie' that Aris and Lora could ride, as well, cousins if around. One time – seems like about five of them rode her to the orchard and ate green apples 'against the rules'! When their parents got home they were given a dose of castor oil. Lesson learned!

Lora loved school and the teachers, Miss Fortner in first and second grades; Mrs. Elizabeth Posey, third and fourth, Mrs. Posey started teaching when she was very young and she even taught the boy that eventually became her husband. Mrs. Posey taught for many years and all of us that grew up in Mayhill had her for first through forth grades, that was called the 'little room'. Classes fifth through eighth were in the 'big room'. When the little white school house was torn down, the bell that we all got to ring, at one time or other, was presented to Mrs. Posey. Sank Tunnell taught fifth through eighth. Such wonderful teachers they were. A lot of happy memories from times spent in the little white school house. It was used for all community activities. Before churches were built, the church of Christ would meet in the mornings, Baptist in the afternoon. Then every so often they would reverse. After they closed the school and all the children started being bused to Cloudcroft, the school was used for a community center and then torn down and a new community center was built where the old out house used to sit.

Elections were held in the school also. I remember one of the politicians came to campaign and while talking he mentioned that he had come through 'Albaququ' and' Sockaro'. He was talking about Albuquerque and Soccoro, New Mexico. Everyone laughed and I always wondered if he misspronounced them for real or on purpose just to get a laugh. There were many school plays there as it had a wonderful stage in the 'big room'. I have a photo of Marie Samford, Dub Cox, John Mershon and Myself that were dressed up like grannies and grandpas when we were about 8 years old. We were dressed for a play that we were in. There were pie or box suppers there. I remember the box suppers so well. They were so much fun for us kids'.

There would be singing conventions where people came from every place. Mr. Miller was a great leader. He could really yodel. When Lora and her family lived on Cox Canyon, across from the Millers, they knew when he went out to do chores – he always yodeled. There were country 'hoe downs', at the old school, that included A.J. Fisher playing the fiddle, and his wife Wanda playing the piano. There were many others, as the mountains was full of good country music performers. Music was a mainstay, and very important part of the mountain peoples lives, whether it was good old country or church songs.

Beth Mahill and Lora were close to the same age, and always together. Kids will be kids and they just knew they were Mr. Tunnell's pets, so they didn't do their workbook assignment to see if he would really take them to the flag pole for some swats with his belt. That day they were not treated any different. He took Lora home so he could talk to Mamie. Ouch! Homework was done after that.

Beth's Parents, Jimmy and Frances Mahill were like second parents to Lora. They always took her to the White Sand Play Days in the spring and to some special movies in Alamogordo.

After grade school, Doggie Scott drove the school bus from Mayhill to Cloudcroft. It was in high school that she met Kenneth. He was known to so many as 'Foosey', a nickname a family friend had given him. He lived on James Canyon across from the Calentine place which is now Cloud Country. Their first date was a ball game in Cloudcroft. On the way from Mayhill they had a flat tire, so they stopped by his home for him to clean up – again! That was when she met his parents, Clay and Josephine, also his sister, Marjorie and Clay Jr, Marjorie and daughter, Martha, were there from New York. Her husband was in the service. Another baby girl, Marye Ann was born while she was there.

Lora and Kenneth were married on March 3, 1944. They lived in Mamie's home on Grandma and Grandpa Brantley's place, for a while, just like so many others that were newly married. It was so far for Kenneth to drive from Mayhill to Cloudcroft so they went to his parents home, on James Canyon, for awhile. Kenneth was working for a logging company driving a log truck from the woods to Cloudcroft. The logs then went by train to Alamogordo, but the train was discontinued not long after that so the Log trucks went on down the hill to the mill.

Kenneth was called for service in World War II with the Navy and was sent to San Diego on October 9, 1944 for six weeks of boot camp. While he was there Lora went to El Cajon, California to meet and stay with her Uncle Bob and Aunt Nellie Frizzell. They spent Thanksgiving with them and soon after Kenneth got two weeks leave. During that leave they spent Christmas at home and went back to California afterward, but by New Years, he had orders to be shipped out.

Lora was on the train again, going home. These were sad times for all of us. Aris was also in the Navy, and Eva's husband, Jack, was in the Army.

After coming home, Lora stayed with Mamie and Grandma Brantley. They were busy sewing for a new baby. She also spent time with her sister Eva and her daughter Velma. Lynda was born May 13, 1945 in Tularosa,

New Mexico. She was born on Mother's Day—what a wonderful gift she was and still is!

Living in Mayhill with a baby was tough during the winter, getting fuel for heat and hauling water for laundry. Lora moved to Alamogordo and rented an apartment from Kenneth's grandmother, Emma Thomason, until Kenneth came home from the Navy. Lynda was eleven months old.

They moved back to the mountains where Kenneth had many different jobs over the years. He worked at Burgett Floral, in fact when needed, Lora helped also. She loved the flowers and Jo Burgett became a very good friend.

They moved to Harvey's Ranch and Game Refuge between Mayhill and Cloudcroft. They liked it up there and the Harveys were such nice people. The Harveys lived in El Paso, Texas.

Kenneth worked for Jimmy Mahill on his farm, and they lived in a house close to the Baptist Church. Steven Wayne was born July 9, 1949 in Artesia, New Mexico while living there in Mayhill. From there they moved to Elk. Kenneth worked for the State Highway Department.

Mamie and Grandma Sarah bought a house in Mayhill after Grandpa Fred died, but Grandma didn't live long after he passed away. Mamie enjoyed her little home, but began having health problems. The doctor said she needed to live in a lower altitude. Eva, Jack and family were living in Carlsbad and Mamie stayed with them until she bought a house large enough for all of them to live in. After a while, Jack found work in Hobbs, New Mexico so they moved there. Kenneth and Lora then moved into the little house in Mayhill and Kenneth worked at Wimsatt's Gas and Grocery, a Planer Mill at Mayhill, and drove a log truck when weather allowed.

Clay and Josephine had the grocery store at Mayhill in the 50's and they first lived below Mayhill on the Chandler place, but bought Mamie's house after Kenneth and Lora decided to move to Carlsbad.

Work was hard to find during the winter in the mountains so they went to Carlsbad and Kenneth found work at the Potash Mines, so they stayed with Mamie until they bought a house and made their home there.

Later Kenneth quit the mines and went into business for himself at a service station where he could do mechanic work, which he really liked to do.

Lora worked at Adkins Fruit and Vegetable Stand when they needed help. The Adkins had lived in the mountains at one time. She also worked at The Medical Arts Lab and XRay in October 1961 to 1979. She had been working there one year when Kenneth was killed in a car wreck, October 22, 1962. She was so thankful that she had a job, it helped her through that tough time.

Steven, Kenneth and Lora's son, passed away on September 1, 1975. He had two children.

Lynda makes her home in California. She has four children and six grandchildren.

Lora, some time after Kenneth's death, married Bill Biggs. They were married quite a few years and he passed away. Lora still lives in their home in Carlsbad.

The Joy family, like others, were pioneers moving toward the west. Richard "Dick" Joy and Ann Elizabeth Compton were married in April of 1856 in Crawford County, Arkansas and left the next day with Dick's family and a wagon train led by Dick's father Riley Joy. They were headed for California but because of the draught of 1856 the Pecos river was the last water going west for many miles. They turned southeast to the Texas Hill Country and settled on the Johnson Fork of the Guadalupe River. Elihu Joy was born here on December 9, 1861. He was the third son out of six boys and three girls born to Dick and Ann.

They were members of the church of Christ and she became Postmistress and a doctor. They were good neighbors and friends to all that passed their way.

Elihu Joy married Nancy Adaline York on May 4, 1884 in Texas. Nancy's parents were William E. York and Martha E. Keith. They were married January 3, 1855 in Hunt County, Texas. The Yorks had come from Tennesse where William was born and the Keith's came from Arkansas where Martha was born. Nancy was born October 6, 1866 and she was the fifth of six children.

Elihu and Nancy lived near Dick and his family and on March 14, 1885 they had a son and named him Harold Eugene. A few months later they joined a wagon train headed for New Mexico where the Yorks had gone a year before in a prairie schooner with a team given to them by Dick. Elihu lead the wagon train. As with all the wagon trains they had some rough times but eventually reached the York home, that was near to where Elk, New Mexico became a town.

A few months went by and they traveled on up into the mountains and built a home on Sixteen Springs Canyon, Lincoln County Territory. They lived there for about twelve years and had five more children. One of those children was William Richard called 'Shorty' born March 11, 1889. When Shorty was ten they moved to a ranch and farm about six miles east of Mayhill, about five and a half miles below the Brantley family, on the Lower Peñasco. Elihu and Nancy had four more children here.

The first wedding in the Joy family here in their newly developing country was Shorty's sister Ella Elizabeth Joy. She married Wiley N. Coe on January 7, 1906. He was the eldest son of Albert M. Coe and Mollie Mahill Coe.

Shorty, who was also called W.R., met and married a Watts girl, Maggie Delene Watts, on July 10, 1910, on the front porch of the Watts old place near Weed. Her father was Thomas 'Tom' Watts.

On May 1, 1884 the wagon train led by William E. York (called Bill) and Martha had a daughter named Mary Luvina, a sister to Nancy A. Joy. Mary married James Madison 'Jim' Dockray in Belton, Bell County, Texas on August 5, 1875. Jim and Mary, somewhere during their traveling, had a baby girl on June 7, 1884 and they named her Mary Elizabeth and called her Lizzie.

Bill York bought and ran the Elk Store for a few years then sold it. He passéd away on June 11, 1904 and Martha followed on March 21, 1907. They are buried in the Elk cemetery.

On May 30, 1904 Joel Warner Curtis passed away at Mayhill, now Otero County, New Mexico and on June 2, 1904 was dropped from the war pension roll.

Tony and Maggie had a house raising on Joel's homestead and most of their neighbors came to help. Within a few days they had a home built. The other children of Joel gave Tony their share in the place and this was their home until Tony could no longer work the place.

An oil painting done by the Author, of Tony and Maggie's home, on the Joel W. Curtis homestead, three miles SW of Mayhill on the Upper Penasco River.

They fenced the house in and part of the land was put into alfalfa, and fenced off. A garden spot, that had been chosen near the ditch, was also fenced. A barn, corrals, smoke house and garage were built through the years. Within the fenced in yard there was an orchard planted of apple, peach, pear and a cherry tree.

Also there was a row of pie cherry bushes planted along the fence next to the road. There were gooseberry bushes near the front yard.

Maggie must have gained the 'good cook' lessons from her mother Sarah because she also could make the best fried chicken you ever eat, and her gooseberry cobblers were as good as Grandma Sarah's.

I loved her meals and when she would cook for the workers, at harvest time, her table would be loaded with everything you could imagine. On Sundays, for 'dinner on the ground' she would always take a big kettle of fried chicken and I was glad to be a 'little kid' as when the line went through there wouldn't be any chicken left. The kids were always fed first!

Maggie also had Hollyhocks and other flowers growing in the corner of the yard and a Virginia Creeper was grown on chicken wire that covered the front of the front porch.

Tony started farming and raised cabbage, corn, carrots and onions to sell at market. He busted broncs in his younger days until the farm started making them a good living.

Maggie became a midwife and delivered a lot of babies until a Doctor Shields come to the Sacramento Mountains. He settled in a little community near Weed called Sacramento.

Maggie was a faithful member of the church of Christ and Tony went with her when they were first married but later quit going.

She was a hard working, loving woman. She had a big black pot that she would build a fire under, and get her lye soap out, that she made after butchering a hog. She would put her clothes in the black pot and use a wooden stick to poke them and swish them around, then she would pick them up with her stick and put them in a galvanized number two wash tub with a rub board and scrub them with her lye soap. Her clothes were always so white and bright.

I remember watching her make cottage cheese out of clabber milk. I loved the clabber milk and she would give me a glass of it. I would put a little salt in it and eat it with a spoon. I also loved the cottage cheese with sugar and milk on it. She never had her hair cut or trimmed and always kept it in a roll on the back of her head.

Grandpa Tony had a special blue granite plate and cup that he eat and drank from. He always ate with his knife and I could never understand how he could keep peas on that knife to get them in his mouth. Also his favorite meal was steak with bread and gravy. He would put sugar on top of his bread and gravy so I decided to try it one day and It was awful tasting.

Tony and Maggie had three sons, all born on their place on the Peñasco. Cara Ivon was born November 21, 1903, Loyd Alton Sr. was born October 25, 1907, and Veolan Elmer born April 21, 1915.

Cara married Ellie Mae Stirman on November 22, 1921 in Avis, New Mexico and they had three sons. Ellie was the daughter of David and Josephine Stirman, another Pioneer family that settled in Lincoln County Territory. Elmer Samuel was born on July 14, 1923 in Perk Canyon, at Weed, New Mexico, Elmer married the daughter of Willie and Laura Dockray, Marjorie Juanita Dockray on September 27, 1940 in Carrizozo, New Mexico.

Willie Dockray was Cleve Dockray's brother.

Ivon Junior was born September 16, 1925 in Mayhill, New Mexico, Ivon married the daughter of Arthur Lee and Effie Corriene 'Vest' Clements, Billy Christine Clements on July 18, 1947. Christine was born May 14, 1931 in Edith, Texas.

Dwain Darrell was born June 9, 1933 in Mayhill, New Mexico and married Christine's sister Peggy Ruth Clements on February 10, 1956 in Lovington, New Mexico. Her birth date was November 1, 1938.

Will Parker wrote a story about his life in a book called (Otero County Pioneer Family Histories) and in it he told several stories, but one was about Uncle Cara and Grandpa Tony.

Will Parker was a brother to John L. Parker that married Leah Posey on December 23, 1922. She was a niece of Maude Posey, who married Will Parker. John L. and Leah had only one child, a daughter, Jaunice, born in 1925 and she married Aris Frizzell, Mamie 'Brantley' Frizzell's son. Aris and Jaunice had two daughters and one son: Hilda 'Frizzell' that married Warren Bain; Teresa 'Frizzell' Mcgouh and Gerald W. Frizzell. Hilda now lives in her mothers and fathers home that was the place her two sets of grandparents had both owned at one time.

Will's and John L.'s parents were Cicero John Parker and Josephine 'Potter' Parker.

They had grown up together and were married in Lampasas, Texas on February 10, 1889. In the summer of that same year, they left Brady, Texas with a wagon train made up of relatives and friends and headed for New Mexico Territory, where they settled in the Weed area. They were farmers and goat ranchers.

In 1907 they bought a farm and ranch on the Peñasco River, four miles east of Mayhill, and moved the family there in March of 1908.

Will's full name was John William Parker and was known by everyone in the area as Will. His father was born in Little Rock, Arkansas and his mother was born in Joplin, Missouri.

He tells that some of the folks they camped with and knew were: the Barkleys, the Watts, the Cadys, the Prathers, the Millers and the Wootsens. A lot of these families his family had known in Texas.

He told of working as a cowboy all the young years of his life and at one time worked on the Flying H Ranch as did almost everyone of my folks at one time or other.

Now, to get back to his tale about Grandpa and Uncle Cara. He states "One time when I was getting ready to make a trip to Roswell. It was winter time and there was a doctor renting a house at Elk, and he wanted some household goods hauled from Roswell. Mr. Cleve asked me if I would go get the doctor's things and I told him I would." He was living on Mule Canyon at that time and there was a lot of dead wood. Tom Jones was a good friend and he and Will had worked together for the Tanniehill Brothers at the Indian reservation. He wanted to go to Roswell with him and he had a good wagon and, four good horses. Tom said, "I can help you haul the doctor's belongings." Will agreed to it and they decided to take some of the wood with them. Earl Van Winkle was also ready to make a trip to Roswell, so they all loaded up with wood and left Mule Canyon.

They went by the Elk Store and Mr. Cleve gave them an order for quite a lot of freight for his store. They left Elk about noon the first day. It was pretty and warm that day and they camped on the head of the Felix the first night. The next day was also warm and that night they camped on the Felix again, just above where the old Weed road came into the Felix, close to the Williamson Waterhole. The next morning when Will woke up he could hear a roaring from the east. It was about four in the morning and the wind was just hitting their camp.

They were camped right down in the Felix, behind a hill, on the west side. When the wind hit the camp the snow was falling just as hard as it could. By daylight the snow was about eight inches deep, and still snowing, coming from the northeast. It wasn't very cold so they decided to get their horses and go on if they could stand to face the snow. They hobbled the horses the night before, but when they went to get them, two of the horses were gone. Tony Curtis and his son, Cara had camped with them, and they still had a team and wagon. Each one of them had two horses.

In all, they had fourteen horses. They found all of the horses close to the camp, except Cara's team. It was snowing so hard that they all decided to wait until it quit before trying to find them.

Earl had a .38 pistol with him and Will took it to hunt rabbits. It began to let up snowing and they could see how to shoot the rabbits so Earl let Will do the shooting as he was the better shot. He shot several in the head and they skinned and cleaned them and cooked them for dinner.

By noon, the sun came out and it got colder. They got the horses and fed them grain, all but Cara's team, which they hadn't found. Tony and Will got on two of the horses bareback and went to hunt for Cara's team. They were camped at the lower end of Flying H country and Will knew every fence corner in the whole area.

Dave Huffman lived at the lower place where Will had lived and there was a fence across the Felix, right at the house and corrals. He thought they would find the team at that gate, but Dave hadn't seen them. By this time, it was getting pretty cold so they looked at all the fence corners and went back to camp. When they got to camp, the horses had been found, down in the creek, below the camp. There was a lot of walnut brush in the Felix near the camp that sheltered the horses and made it hard to see them.

They stayed another night there and the next morning it was clear and real cold. They got ready and started on their way. It was so cold they all had to walk to keep warm.

Cara was just a young boy about thirteen or fourteen years old, so he didn't get out to walk at first. They went quite a ways and Cara still hadn't gotten out of the wagon. Will was in the lead so he stopped and waited until they all caught up and told Tony he would have to get Cara out of the wagon and make him walk, if he didn't Cara would freeze to death.

Will was the only one of the bunch that had on warm clothes. He stated that "The rest of them didn't have enough clothes to wad a shotgun."

Will had been to Roswell with his Papa a short time before and had ridden in that country so much that he knew it was zero or below by the way he was dressed. Tony and Tom Jones had just light clothes, as did Earl. Earl had on a dress coat that didn't have a button on it and he was facing the northeast wind.

There were five wagons and Cara was in the back wagon. Will got him out and he was so cold he could hardly walk at first, so he took him with him. He got mad at Will at first but after awhile he said "you saved my life." They kept walking all day that day.

They stopped at noon at one of the campgrounds where there was a bluff that faced the south. They built a fire and ate dinner and all got warm and full of strong coffee. After their meal they continued on and made it to Carlos Well that night.

They corralled the wagons in a circle, looking for a way to keep warm and tied their horses to the wagon's wheels and built a big fire in the middle of the circle. They all put their beds close together around the fire to stay warm.

They had three wagons loaded with wood but Tony and Cara had two wagons loaded with cabbage and Tony also had a stack of potatoes in one wagon that he was taking to some of his relatives that lived in Roswell. The cabbage and potatoes froze solid.

They ate the rest of their chuck for breakfast that morning, except the coffee, of which they only had a little left and continued on until noon. They were about twenty five miles from Roswell and the wind was blowing really hard so they stretched up a big heavy wagon sheet for protection and built a fire. They broke the ice in a water trough and made coffee and boiled some of Tony's frozen potatoes. After they ate they went on into town that night.

Tony and Cara went to the PV Wagon Yard. Tony said "I'll get a shed to put the wagons under." He thought some of his cabbages might not be frozen. Earl, Tom and Will went to the Roswell Trading Company Yard.

The wind quit blowing that night and the next morning it was snowing again but Earl and Tom went on out and tried to sell the wood. They went all over Roswell but didn't sell any. It snowed all that day and the next day it cleared and turned cold. This was the second day they had been there.

That night it got down to twenty two degrees below Zero. The third day they tried again to sell the wood but they still couldn't sell any. They thought when the cold storm hit, they would be able to sell the wood like hotcakes but it just didn't happen.

Will never did pull his wagon out of the yard so when they were ready to start home, they had to gather up what freight they were going to haul for Mr. Cleve, he asked the yard man if he would buy the wood and he said he'd give him fifteen dollars for it. Will said, "You can just have it.", and unloaded it. When the man figured up the feed bill he owed him fifteen dollars and five cents. Will gave him a nickel and thanked him and they started getting ready to pull out.

Tony lost all his cabbage, as it all froze, so he couldn't sell them. They left Roswell after dinner and it had started warming up some, but was still cold traveling. From Made Tank to Elk there was quite a lot of snow on the ground and it took three days to go back.

The second day out of Roswell, they stopped at the Parker Flat Windmill to water the horses. 'Old Negro' Add was staying there for the Diamond Cattle Company. Will was the only one he knew, and when he recognized him he came out and talked for a while, while the horses watered. Will had worked with Add at the Diamond several years before.

It was around January 20, 1918 when they arrived back home.

Will Parker became a well known Sheriff throughout the whole region. He went into the Sheriffs office in January of 1939 in Otero County. He left it on December 31, 1946. Ray Prather was one of his Deputies. He was good help and wanted to run for the office the next term, which Will was glad to see. He knew Ray would make a good sheriff as he treated everybody the same. Will was a very well liked person also and helped a lot of people in his day.

Will remembered one time in the pioneer days in the Weed country when it was getting pretty dry in the early summer and everybody was out of feed. Horses were poor and had lots of ticks. People would mix up sulphur and salty meat grease and rub it all over the horses. One day an old man came to their house and his dad had a white horse he had put this solution on. This old man asked "what is on that white horse." Will's dad said "It's sulphur and grease." The old man told him "If it rains that will kill your horses." Will's dad retorted "I don't care as the ticks are eating them up anyway." It started raining a short time after that and rained everyday for a month, but it didn't kill the horses.

Loyd Alton Curtis, the second son of Tony and Maggie was born on the Curtis Homestead on October 25, 1907.

Loyd married Eunice Neva Joy on May 28, 1927 in Roswell, New Mexico. Eunice was the daughter of W.R. 'Shorty' Joy and Maggie Delene 'Watts' Joy.

Loyd and Eunice lived on the Curtis place on the Peñasco River in a house upon the hill a short distance from the main house. Loyd worked at various jobs, as a cowboy for W.R. Joy, his father–in–law, and he also homesteaded a section of land on the Felix joining the township that W.R. and his brother Fussy Joy had homesteaded earlier.

They moved onto the land and bought and started raising a few goats. There were no fences there and had not built any so they had to stay with and herd them day and night. They had some very good dogs that helped them out though.

They moved back to Mayhill and Loyd drove the school bus back and forth to Cloudcroft for two or three years.

After that Loyd bought land in Mayhill then built and ran a Garage for a while. My dad worked for him for a short time as a mechanic. Some time later he built and ran a bar that had their home in the back. Later he added a Filling Station to his holdings.

He loved horses and was gone a lot to Ruidosa and the horse races. Eunice ran the bar when he was gone.

They had three children: the first was Loyd Alton Jr. 'L.A.' as we called him. He was born September 5, 1930 in the same house that his dad was born in. He married Fidelia Sue Willburn, in Carrizozo, New Mexico on May 20, 1950. She was born January 11, 1934 in Hope, New Mexico. Her parents were Lloyd Lavern and Mertha Erma 'Buckner' Willburn.

L.A. and Sue had four children: the first one was Jerry Dean born February 24, 1951, Jerry never married and died of a heart attack on July 9, 2005. Second child was Jackie Lane born September 21, 1953, he married Elizabeth Gallegos and they had a son Geramy Ray. Elizabeth died in 2005 and he has remarried. The third child was Rocky Dale born July 30, 1955 in Ft. Sumner, New Mexico. He married Lori Lynn Lachniet on June 22, 1980 in Alto, Michigan. Her parents are Roger Allen and Maureen Kay 'Delaney'. He was born on April 6, 1935 and she was born on September 18, 1938 and they were married on June 22, 1957. Rocky and Lori have two boys; Kaleb Loyd and Kanon Matthew. The fourth child was Dolly Sue born June 4, 1963, in Soccorro, New Mexico.

Sue and L.A. were divorced when Dolly was very young.

Sue passed away in 2005, and he married Merryann 'Dusty' Peterson on May 31, 1986.

L.A. remembered the days when they lived about three and half miles from the school and there were no buses at that time so he rode a horse for the first three years until he was eight years old.

Loyd and Eunice's second child was Murrell Dean and he married Wilda Marie Scranton in Roswell, N.M. on August 31,1957. She was born on August 9, 1937 in Wyoming they were divorced on May 10, 1983. Murrell passed away on April 22, 1992 and is buried in Alamogordo, N.M.

Murrell and Wilda had seven children: Faron Murrell, born December 20, 1958 in Roswell, N.M. and he married Jennifer Wilson on July 25, 2980 in Ruidosa, N.M.. They were divorced in October of 1983 and he married Donna Gunter on October 5, 1986 in Ruidosa, N.M.

Rebecca Marie was born December 24, 1959 in Roswell, N.M. and she married Larry Baker on December 31, 1987 in Seminole, TX. They were divorced on July 18, 2000.

Brenda Joy was born in Roswell, N.M. on March 12, 1961 and married Carlos Lawrance Payton on July 7, 1978 in Seminole. He was born on November 23, 1959.

Perry Loyd was born on July 5, 1962 in Roswell, N.M. and married Denice Jean Cunningham on March 8, 1982 in Alamogordo, N.M.. Her date of birth was July 16, 1960 in Friona, Texas.

Tammy Merlene was born on July 29, 1963 in Roswell, N.M. and she married Branson Leon Tefertiller on July 30, 1983 in Seminole, TX. He was born on February 9, 1963

Ferlin Webb was born on May 22, 1966 in Roswell, N.M. and he married Connie Lynn Hughs on July 22, 1988 in Seminole, TX. She was born on October 30, 1962.

Danny Watts was born on February 24, 1968 and married Tonya Denise Davidson on March 14, 1998 in Seminole, TX. She was born on July 28, 1965.

The third child of Loyd and Eunice was Marilyn Joy, born on April 10, 1932 in Mayhill, N.M. She married Charles Edwin McMurry on December 31, 1958. He was born on September 13, 1940 in Lamesa, TX.Charles and Marilyn had two children: Rodney Charles, born on

April 25, 1961 in Alamogordo, N.M. and he married Kimberly Susanne Ashmore. She was born on April 1, 1967.

The second child of Charles and Marilyn was Rhonda Gaye 'Missy' born on September 9, 1963 and she married Jay Howard Yerkey. He was born on October 25, 1963 also.

Some of the things Marilyn remembered was a favorite time in her formative years with her dad when she got to go turkey hunting with him. He made a turkey caller from a piece of slate and a piece of wood, about 5 inches long that was carved very round and smooth with a corn cob handle.

He would almost always get an answer and he would always get a turkey for their Thanksgiving dinner. Most of his turkey hunting was done in Curtis Canyon, sometimes in other areas around the mountains close to Mayhill. Even though her dad was somewhat hard of hearing, he could hear a turkey call from a mile away. She thought that was 'selective hearing'.

She remembered the time her dad killed a bear and brought it home. They were all standing around beside the bar, at their home while they were taking pictures of it. The bear happened to move slightly from being positioned for pictures and Jerry, L.A.'s son was just a little tyke, climbed to the top of Loyd's shoulders in a matter of seconds. He wanted nothing to do with that thing.

Loyd loved to rodeo. He had a horse named Wonder that he used to rope on. The old horse trailer he had was just a trailer with wooden slat sides and no top. Marilyn remembered going with her dad and mother, one time, to Alamogordo. They had to travel the old Cloudcroft road that was just gravel, and go through the tunnel (this was before the tunnel was enlarged). Loyd would stop and Marilyn would get in the trailer and hold Wonder's head down so they could drive through with him.

She loved going to Roswell with her mother. They would have to go at least once a month for supplies for the bar. It seemed like that was the only time she got to be alone with her. She can remember getting to what they called the 'bear cave' where the pavement ended going southwest to Mayhill and always saying to her mother "Can we turn around and go back to Roswell?"

Fond memories of Grandpa and Grandma Curtis are still with her. She stated that "I would go up and spend a lot of time there and my cousin Deloris (Kay) and I were always together there, playing either paper dolls or combing Grandpa's hair while he was sitting in his rocker playing his fiddle. He would spit tobacco in the fireplace, sometimes missing and that would really upset Grandma. She stated "I can still hear her saying in a very agitated voice; 'Tony'...."

Her fondest memories of Grandma are the times seeing her sitting in her rocking chair, with her Bible and study book on her lap, doing her Bible lesson. She said "I remember her reading out of the book of Lamentations and she always made it to get me and take me to worship services every Sunday and to Wednesday night Bible study. You might say whenever the door was open Grandma Maggie was there. Marilyn's sentiments were "If it had not been for her love for me in seeing that I was taught about God, I would not have known about his teachings or his word or even what the inside of a church building was like. I'm very thankful and grateful for her dedication and for the model she set at being the godly woman she was, a woman that loved the Lord Jesus Christ with all her heart and soul."

Cara and Ellie's oldest son Elmer was born on upper Perk Canyon and after several moves with his parents they moved across the street from the Mayhill Store and Café.

His dad Cara, at one time, owned the first Phillips 66 Station that was built in Mayhill, and Elmer worked for him, before and after school.

The only telephone line in the area was the Forest Service phone with a connection at Mayhill. If an emergency call of any nature came in for some one in the area, Cara would send Elmer to deliver the message. Elmer was so small Cara had to put an old fashioned wooden coke box behind him, in the seat, and one under him, so he could see out of the windshield. Elmer was much younger than children that are supposed to be driving but at that time there were very few cars and the roads were all either gravel or just dirt. Elmer always delivered the message and returned safely.

Elmer loved to hunt from a very early age and was taught safety and responsibility with fire arms. He became a very good marksman and brought home game to eat when he went out.

Elmer married Marjorie on September 27, 1940. She was born about three miles south of Mayhill on the place known then as the York Place. Her parents were William 'Willie' Hiram and Laura Ellen Marshall

Dockray. She moved with her parents and siblings to the Pecos Valley and lived near Hagerman and Dexter for a few years then they moved back to the mountains. They first lived on her Uncle Cleve Dockray's place near Elk, New Mexico and later back to the Mayhill area.

Marjorie finished grade school at Mayhill and completed High School at Cloudcroft. One indelible memory of hers when she was going to school at Elk was when her brother got his arm broken.

They walked, maybe one and a half miles, to school but some times the Bates children would let part of them double with them on horseback and they had one horse they would double or even triple on. This day Robert, Billy and Marj were on their horse and about half way there she didn't want to go any further. They had Marj get off and they were going to make the horse go. Well, the horse had other ideas, and after a very short rodeo Robert was on the ground with a broken arm. Billy went back home to get help while Robert and Marj sat on the side of the road, with her crying. Robert looked at her and asked "What are you crying for? It's my arm that's broken."

Elmer and Marj had two children: the first child was Wanda Carolyn and she was born January 29, 1942. She married Howard George Laire Jr. on August 13, 1966 and they had three children, Nicole Michelle, David Tatanka, and Carolyn Lorraine.

Their second child was Cara William "Bud" Curtis and Bud married Paula Kay Hammond on August 28, 1965 and they have two children, Julie Jil and Tate William.

After living a short time on the Flying H Ranch in 1941, they moved to Fabens, Texas and Elmer operated a dairy for his Uncle Andrew for a while then worked at the Meyers Company where Andrew was the manager. On their move to Fabens they put all of their belongings in a Model A Ford Roadster with no top and drove there in August, with the sun beating down on them without mercy. Believe it that the roads were not like today, no pavement, just scraped out wide enough between the mesquite covered sand dunes for cars to meet and pass. About the only place they could see was straight ahead or straight up.

By that time Marj was pregnant with Wanda so they stopped in El Paso, Texas to see a doctor who would care for her through the birth.

They moved to Alamogordo in late 1942 where Elmer would carry the mail to Cloudcroft and Mayhill until he went into the Navy in June of 1944. Bud was born while they lived in Alamogordo.

Just before Elmer left for the Navy he moved the children and Marj back to Mayhill so they would be near their parents. After the end of the war Elmer was discharged in February 1946. They then moved to Roswell and he went to work for the U.S. Postal Service from which he retired in July 1978. During their stay in Roswell, Marj worked for the Green Stamp Company for seven years and fourteen years as office manager for the Gibson Discount company. The next day after Elmer retired they returned to Mayhill. They had been buying the Old Curtis homestead on time payments for several years and also the adjacent Barkley place that had been part of the original homestead. They chose to build a new home on the Barkley portion of what Marj is still living on. The house is built in almost the same spot that Cecil Barkley had his house. After much consideration they downsized their original plans for the house so they would be debt free and not have to worry about payments and more. Their home is in a beautiful setting and because she loved flowers and a lawn she has been able to make it an admired place.

Elmer was very happy doing the kind of things he loved, raising cattle, horses and going hunting. He also bought an old tractor with a front end loader and back hoe. He worked for other people building roads, putting in septic systems, just about anything he could with the tractor. He really enjoyed helping people. He was assistant fire chief for a time with the Mayhill Volunteer Fire Department. He died of cancer on September 10, 1994.

Veolan Elmer Curtis was the third child born to Maggie and Tony. He married Silvia Vera Watson in 1938. Silvia was the daughter of Mr. Watson, that Aunt Nola married, from a previous marriage. She ran away with another man about one year after they were married and he divorced her on June 27, 1939.

On June 27, 1939 he married Carrie Lou Ella 'Williams' 'Showers'. Her parents were Richard Colton and Minnie Ola 'Bullard' Williams and she was born June 9, 1921 in Ore City, Upshur County, Texas. She was the youngest of 13 children born to Minnie. When she was eleven years old she married a man named Clyde Emmit Showers. Richard James was born to them on July 31, 1934 and Minnie Louise was born on December

24, 1936. Clyde was much older than Carrie and he liked to hobo on rail cars and travel the country. He would drag Carrie along with him and they happened to be in Zealand, Michigan when James 'Jim' was born. He then started taking Carrie back to her mother and leaving her but show up once in awhile and while he was away one of these times Louise was born. Minnie her mother was living in a town on the outskirts of Las Cruces, New Mexico called Fairacres.

Minnie had moved to New Mexico because her son Julius 'Jude' Williams had moved to New Mexico and he could help her. At the time Louise was born, Minnie and Carrie were picking cotton to make a living. Jude hired on with Jimmy Mayhill as a foreman on his ranch and he moved Minnie and Carrie to a worker's house on the ranch as Carrie now had two babies to care for and they were not going to have a job after the cotton season was over. This is when Veolan met Carrie and after dating for a time they were married.

Veolan raised Jim and Louise as if they were his own and then on April 18, 1940 they had Deloris Kay their only child together. Kay was born on the Curtis Homestead.

Maggie named Kay from a radio program she always listened to. On this radio show there was a woman named Kay that owned a ranch and she had a lady that cooked and kept the house for her named Deloris and those two names were put together for her name.

Deloris Kay is the Author of this book!

Veolan and Carrie were married in Tony and Maggie's home by a Minister of the Gospel by the name of S.T. Montgomery and their two witness's were Roy and Perrene 'Brantley' Kemper.

The newly weds then moved into the little house on the hill just above Tony and Maggie's and lived there until the summer of 1952 when work was scarce in the Mayhill area and Veolan went to Carlsbad and stayed with his Aunt Mamie until he found a job at the PCA potash mine.

Veolan then went back to Mayhill and moved Carrie and Kay to Carlsbad. Louise was already married and on her own and Jim decided to stay with his Uncle Jude and Aunt Lois in Alamagordo, so he could graduate from Cloudcroft, as it was his senior year in school.

Veolan eventually rented Aunt Mamie's house on Fox Street and she had a small house in the back of it that she lived in and they lived there until PCA started laying off hands in December of 1957.

At this time they packed up and moved back to Mayhill and stayed with Tony and Maggie until they rented one of the camp house apartments. It seems a lot of our family that left the mountains eventually moved back.

Carrie went to work for the Thomasons in their grocery store and part time worked in the Western Wear Store. Veolan was still looking for a job.

Tony became very sick and was taken to Carlsbad and the doctor put him in the hospital. He had cancer and he died in the hospital on May 25, 1958, this was about the same day Kay graduated from High School.

While in the hospital he gave my folks money to buy me a graduation dress. It was blue and I felt so beautiful in it. He was so special to me. He let me drive his tractor one time, while sitting on his lap. He wasn't paying very good attention and I managed to run into the fence between his place and Cecil Barkley's. It took a good days work for him and my dad to repair it.

Grandpa Tony had a horse named 'Ole Streak'. She had a white steak all the way down her face and was such a gentle mare that us kids could walk all around her feet, behind her, under her, etc. and she would never flinch. I can't remember not ever riding her so I must have been very small the first time. Grandpa saddled her often for me to ride, and one thing I remember about her. As gentle as she was if you were riding any where close to a tree she would try to rub you off with it. I loved those days and my grandparents so very much.

After his funeral Veolan, Carrie and Kay moved in with Maggie.

Maggie had a doctors appointment in Alamogrodo so Carrie, Ellie, Kay and Maggie all started to Alamogordo on August 1, 1958 with Kay driving.

It was drizzling rain that morning and shortly after passing the spring on Cloudcroft hill, a few miles out of Cloudcroft, the windows started to fog over. The defrosters were not working and it was hard for Kay to see so Carrie took a Kleenex and started wiping the windshield when the right tire slipped off the pavement.

Kay over corrected by jerking the steering wheel and the car started skidding. It turned around with the front end headed back up the hill and went off of a seventy five foot embankment and rolled over once with the front of the car on top of a barbed wire fence.

Maggie died, on the way down the hill, in the Ambulance and Carrie was taken to the hospital but died a short time later. Ellie and Kay were taken to the hospital and Ellie was ok to go home but Kay was in the hospital for several days with cuts, lacerations, and broken bones.

I was unable to attend the funerals of my mother and grandmother, but my cousin Troy from California, my mother's sister Myrtle's son, came to the hospital and they let me go with him, in a wheel chair, to the funeral home to say goodbye.

Veolan and Carrie were faithful members of the church of Christ all the years they were together. Veolan led singing, and taught a Bible class for several years in the Mayhill Church.

Veolan then married Anna Pauline 'Worley' 'Vick' on November 20, 1958, Pauline was born as Anna Pauline Honycut and was adopted by Roy and Edna 'Posey' Worley when she was a baby. She was born in El Paso, Texas on August 29, 1932.

After Roy and Edna could no longer take care of Pauline, their daughter Lois 'Worley' Williams and her husband Jude Williams (Carrie's brother) took her to raise. She was about six years old. She grew up with Lois and Jude's children so they thought of her like a sister. Jude and Lois had three sons; Lester Eugene, Glen Richard and James Charles (we all called him Charley).

Pauline had been married before to Jimmy Vick and had a daughter Lois Ann Vick, born on October 17, 1976 in Alamogordo, New Mexico. Veolan also raised Lois Ann part of time but most of the time she was living with Uncle Jude and Aunt Lois. Veolan and Pauline had a daughter, Janet Faye, born August 13, 1959 in Alamogrodo, New Mexico.

Veolan had no children with Silvia.

Richard James known as 'Jimmy' or 'Jim' married Valarie Fay Quick on February 18, 1953 in Alamogordo, New Mexico. Her parents were Marcus and Ola Quick. She was born on July 14, 1935. They were divorced about 1975 in Farmington, New Mexico. He married a woman named Judy and they were divorced sometime around early 1980's. Jim and Val had six children; Wanda Faye was born on October 4, 1954 in Alamogordo; Darrell Ray was born April 4, 1956 in Alamogordo; Donna Kay was born on March 30, 1958 in Alamogordo; James Allen was born on January 25, 1961 in Alamogordo; Carrie Edna was born on November 2, 1962, and Dennis Lee was born on May 1, 1965 in Alamogordo.

Louise married William Andrew 'W.A.' Honeycutt on March 29, 1952 and they divorced February 14, 1956. She married Richard LeRoy Grabbe on March 10, 1956 and they divorced July 26, 1971. She then Married George William Tice on November 23, 1976 and divorced September 27, 1984. Married Norman Allen Schall July 18, 1984, divorced March 23, 1994. Married W.A. Honeycutt in 1994 in Monte vista, Colorado and divorced in 2007.

Louise and W.A. had two children; Juanitta Louise Honeycutt and she was born on July 10, 1953 in Carlsbad, David Wayne Honeycutt and he was born on September 1, 1954 in Carlsbad.

Louise and Dick Grabbe had two children; Clarice Starr Grabbe and she was born January 15, 1959 and she died March 29, 1959, Alvena Pearl Grabbe and she was born on March 18, 1962.

Louise and George Tice adopted Anthony 'Tony' Wayne Tice as a baby in 1977 and he was born November 30, 1976 in Durango, Colorado. Louise, Tony and his family are all members of the church of Christ on Airport Road in Hot Springs, Arkansas.

Deloris Kay married Billy Darrell Morgan on September 24, 1958 and they were divorced on September 20, 1963. They had no children.

Darrell's parents were Joseph Willie 'Bill' Morgan and he was born in Elawah, North Carolina on March 15, 1904 to Thomas and Rebecca Morgan. He came to New Mexico in 1927 and went to work for South West lumber Company, in Marcia Canyon, which was owned and operated by Louis Carr. That is where he met Ruby Alma Williams, where she was working at a cookhouse, at the log camp. She was born in Enid, Arkansas on July 2, 1914.

Her parents were Joe and Onie Bell 'Pace' Williams. They were married June 17, 1929 in Alamogordo and they moved some different places but ended back in Mayhill in 1942. They had three children: Allene 'Morgan' Clayton that married Charlie Clayton, son of Allen and Onie 'Scott' Clayton; the second child was Melvin 'Red' Morgan that is now married to Barbara; and Billy Darrell Morgan. Darrell was born in 1937.

Carrie and Ruby were very good friends during all the years in Mayhill until the death of Carrie.

Kay Married Jerry Lee Bice on September 23, 1963 in Carlsbad, New Mexico and divorced on February 12, 1975 in Farmington, New Mexico.

His parents were Joseph Longstreet and Dottie Annita 'Hale' Bice. He was born in 1942 in Bakersfield, California. Jerry and Kay had two sons: Jimmie Lee, born in Tucumcari, N.M. on June 12, 1964; Joe Elden, born in Victory, TX on November 29, 1967.

Kay married again to Richard Paul Kowalewski on September 12, 1981 in Breckenridge, Colorado and they were divorced in June of 1986. Rich had two daughters when they married. Brenda Sue, born February 19, 1969 in Nebraska; Ann Marie, born May 13, 1972 in Nebraska. Their mother was Ellan Evelyn Olsen.

These girls were six and nine when Kay married their father and as far as she is concerned they are her 'daughters'. She loves them as though they were.

Kay then married Jerry Keith Ward on February 14, 1988 in Monte Vista, Colorado, at the Central church of Christ by Boyd Glover (minister). Jerry's date of birth is April 30, 1934 in Denver, Colorado to Granville Willard and Alice Mae 'Camby' Keith.

His birth name was Granville Alvin Keith. He and his brother were placed in an orphannage in Denver when they were very young and he was adopted by George Albian and Muriel Francis 'Bennett' Ward just short of his sixth birthday in 1940 and was raised on their ranch west of Saguache, Colorado. Jerry and Kay are faithful members of the church of Christ in Mountain Pine, Arkansas.

Jim, Louise and I all grew up on the Curtis Homestead. We had a hard but wonderful life. My Dad and Mother were as faithful members of the church of Christ as was Grandma Curtis. My dad would drive Grandma and Grandpa's car when going to services and Grandma would ride with us. We would stop at Uncle Loyd and Aunt Eunice's and pick Marilyn up on our way.

When it came harvest time everyone in the family had to be involved. We all had hoes and were in the fields with the adults hoeing weeds or harvesting the produce. You didn't get distracted when hoeing and hoe up a vegetable or you were reprimanded. You had to pay attention and work hard or else!

Jim graduated from the eighth grade in June of 1949. He then rode the bus to Cloudcroft for the next three years to attend high school. In 1952 when our parents had to move to get work Jim went to live with Uncle Jude and Aunt Lois in Alamogordo so he could graduate with his friends. The sad part of this was, he did not get to graduate because he did not have enough credits. They waited to tell him this after he had his senior and graduation photos made and was a few weeks from graduation.

Jim went to work in construction with Loyd Curtis for a time. He worked at a service station, and at one time Jude ran a taxi service in Alamogordo, and Jim drove taxi for him.

He mostly worked as foreman on construction jobs in and around the State of New Mexico, and some out of state jobs, for many years. Among his many jobs, one of these was the Gorge Bridge between Taos and Tres Piedras, New Mexico, and the Hutton Plaza in Farmington, New Mexico. Eventually he was a partner in a construction corporation, Re: Showers Construction Co. Inc. based in Farmington, New Mexico.

Jim ended up loosing his company because missmanagement of money by his second wife. This was like a last straw for him. He had never gotten over the loss of his mother and then to loose his company was devastation for him. He kept on trying though, and he and his wife Judy moved to the Elkhorn just out of Fairplay, Colorado. He was not able to find work and they had to move back to Farmington. He divorced Judy, and was drinking heavy during all this time. He took his own life on August 8, 1980 and was buried close to his mother in the Peñasco Cemetery at Mayhill, New Mexico.

Louise moved to Arkansas near Kay and her husband Jerry.

She lived alone for about a year and her son Wayne moved down from Arizona and built a home. He moved her in with him and she has lived with him for two years. She is now moving into her own home that Wayne and his wife purchased for her to live in. She is happy and a faithful member of the church of Christ on Airport Road.

Louise's youngest son and his wife, Tony and Erica, and their four children also live close to the family here in Arkansas.

Bettie Elizabeth Brantley was Fred and Sarah's eighth child and she was born July 16, 1897 at Mayhill, New Mexico. She married John McQuarter Fleming on August 2, 1914. He was born December 10, 1888 and raised in Wills Canyon at Weed, New Mexico.

His parents were Thomas Farr and Tulula Fleming. He was the sixth child born to this couple.

His father was a rancher all his life except for owning a store in Weed at one time. Tom's family moved from Weed to Piñon to ranch.

John also became a rancher raising cattle, horses and goats. He and Bettie homesteaded west of Tom's ranch (southwest of Piñon) and they lived here until John's death on November 24, 1945. After Bettie could no longer care for herself she went to the Lakeview Christian Home in Carlsbad, New Mexico until her death on August 14, 1984. She and John are buried at the Peñasco cemetery, Mayhill, New Mexico.

My parents told me a story about going to visit Uncle John and Aunt Bettie, one time, when I was barely walking. They all went out to see the new baby goats. Mother put me down by one of the babies and I grabbed hold of it and wouldn't let go. It was pulling me along with it as it walked but I held on for dear life. Uncle John said "Veolan, that goat belongs to Deloris so you take it home with her."

They took the goat home with us and was he ever a pain. I loved him dearly but he was into everything so finally they took him down to the Flying H Ranch where Uncle Loyd and Aunt Eunice were working and they watched over him for me and for about two years, at shearing time, they would give me the money from his wool. Mother saved the money and bought me a gold heart locket with a matching bracelet with my initials engraved on them. Every time I looked at the jewelry I would think of how I came about getting them.

John and Bettie had three children. Number one was Nada Ilene and she was born May 11, 1915 . She married John Bushnell Creed on October 25, 1943 in Santa Fe, New Mexico. Their second child was Leslie Gilbert and he was born June 13, 1917. He fought in World War II and was captured and was in the Bataan Death March.

Leslie spent a long time in a horrid prison camp. He never got over what happened to him and his comrades in the camp. I remember some, telling stories about them being in cages that they couldn't stand up in and the filth in them. They were not fed for long periods of time and mice would run through the cages and they would catch them and eat them to keep from starving to death.

Leslie was released from the prison camp when the war ended and after coming back home he married Maryellen Helen Stillwell on December 30, 1945 in Alamogordo, New Mexico.

Benny Vernon Fleming was born February 3, 1925. He married Marjorie Pearl Potter, on February 6, 1946, in Tularosa, New Mexico. She was born May 1, 1928.

In 1957, Benny and Marjorie bought the balance of the Don Lee (the Sacramento River Ranch) ranch that wasn't taken when McGregor Range purchased all the ranch land. They live there for twenty two years. In August 1969 they purchased the homestead of his parents, from his mother. In 1979 they sold the Sacramento River Ranch and moved back to the old homestead ranch where Marjorie was still living in 2003.

They had five children, the first one was Benny Vernon Jr. and he was born January 22, 1947.

Their second child was Marjorie Elaine and she was born September 6, 1948. Their third child was Margarett Ellen, born on September 6, 1948.

Marjorie Elaine and Margarett Ellen were twins. Number four child was John Thomas and he was born on January 21, 1956 . The fifth child was James Everett and he was born on May 1, 1958 .

Nola Irue Brantley was the tenth child of Fred and Sarah Brantley. She was born on September 12, 1904 at Mayhill, New Mexico. She married Edward Watson on May 27, 1929. They had three children: Jamie Watson that married James O. Verman and they had three boys and two girls; Hillard Watson that married Joyce Taylor and they had two girls and one boy; Willard Watson that married Dorothy Creek and they had two girls and one boy.

Nola had gone somewhere and when she came home she found Mr. Watson dead in his chair.

When Darrell Morgan and I were married we moved to Artesia for awhile and Aunt Nola lived there. I visited with her a lot and came to love her very much. She later went into a nursing home in Roswell, New Mexico and sometime around 1989 Jerry and I went by to visit with her on our way to a Curtis Stirman family reunion in Curtis Canyon. I had taken some old photo's that Grandma and Grandpa Curtis had given me to see if she could tell me who some of them were. I so enjoyed visiting with her again.

Jerry was raised a cowboy on a homestead ranch in Saguache Colorado and dressed the part (still does). He, for many years has worn a straw cowboy hat painted blue (that's another story to tell) and his cowboy boots, blue jeans and western style shirt. When we walked into the nursing home there was a little lady sitting in her wheel chair near the door and when she looked up and saw him she got the brightest smile on her face and asked him "Did you tie your horse up outside?" We all had a good laugh over that.

After Mr. Watson passed away Aunt Nola married a man named Andrews.

I have no other dates or information for this family. I know that sometime after Jerry and I visited with her she passed away there in the nursing home.

The eleventh and last child born to Fred and Sarah was Elza Hillard Brantley. He was born on October 14, 1908 at Mayhill, New Mexico. He married Wilma Scott in Mayhill, New Mexico. They had three children: William Scott Brantley that died; Zelma Brantley that married Walter Bradley and they had three girls and one boy; E.J. Brantley married Martie and had two boys. On March 1, 2001 at Eva Grice's funeral I talked to E.J. for a few minutes and his wife's name was Helen. I don't have the information on what happened to Martie.

I never was around Uncle Elza and Aunt Wilma very much but I remember Aunt Wilma being a cut up. She loved to joke and laugh with everyone. In 1958, When Grandpa Tony went into the hospital in Carlsbad, she was an RN there and she kept his spirits up by joking around with him all the time, on her shift.

E.J. was a horse trainer, during the years we lived in Carlsbad, at a big ranch between Carlsbad and Artesia. He was very tall, I think about six feet four inches and he used to visit us some and we went out once to the ranch where he worked and watched him with a horse he was training. He passed away shortly after Eva's funeral. Zelma's husband passed away a few years ago and she is living in an Assisted living Apartment complex in Carlsbad and is a faithful member of the church of Christ. Many years have come and gone since these pioneers traveled our plains and mountains and forged out their lives with the sweat of their brows, and calloused, rough hands. They fought heat and cold, Indians and bad men but they were a good stock of people that made our country what it is today. The history books are filled with people like this but this is my family, my people and I'm so very proud to come from such folk. God calls his faithful servants the salt of the earth and I know that most of these people were just that.

Bibliography

1. Arkansas' Mexican War Soldiers, By: Desmond Walls Allen; Arkansas Research

2. Charles Goodnight 'Cowman and Plainsman', By: J. Evetts Haley

3. Cousins By The Dozens, By: Margaret Ward

4. DareDevils All (The Texan Mier Expedition, 1842 – 1844, By: Joseph Milton Nance

5. Copy of Affidavit from Joel W. Curtis for The Estate of T. Dawson

6. John Barkley Dawson 'Pioneer, Cattleman, Rancher, By: Delphine Dawson Wilson

7. Otero County Pioneer Family History (Vol. 2 *Published by the Tularosa Basin Historical Society, Alamogordo, New Mexico 1985*)

8. The Chases of Cimarron, By: Ruth W. Armstrong

9. The New Handbook of Texas, (In six volumes) Volume 4 (Austin – The Texas State Historical Association, 1996)

10. The Story of Texas, 'Text By: John Edward Weems' Compiled By: Ron Stone

11. Huntin' Memories, By: Virginia Stanbrough

12. Kemper Genealogy – Vol. 5 1635 – 1984) provided By: Janette Bice Rielman; Further Information Provided by:

1. A time line for Joel Curtis, compiled by: Jody Weldy

2. A copy of affidavit from Joel W. Curtis for the Estate of T. Dawson

3. Information told by Zenas Curtis and shared by: Marilyn Decker

4. The Albuquerque Genealogical Society: Records of the Methodist Episcopal Church (1867 – 1918)

5. News Paper Articles: The History of Mayhill, by: Pat Rand (Museum of Otero County, New Mexico)

   The CurrentArgus, Carlsbad, N.M. Tuesday, January 6, 1987

   The Cloudcroft Silver Lining, Cloudcroft, New Mexico

   The White Man, Weatherford, Parker County, Texas: A notice in Saturday, September 15, 1860 issue.

   The Library of Congress (A century of Lawmaking for a New Nation: US Congressional Documents and Debates 1774 – 1875)

   Journal of The January 13, 1874, page 234

   House of Representatives February 1, 1869, Page 241

6. Primitive Baptist Church and Family History: Research Assistance for the State of New Mexico Church's: Bethel (1874)

7. U.S. Records and Pensions Office 'War Department' Commissioner of Pensions: for Joel W. Curtis

8. U.S. War Archives: Mexican War: Papers for Joel Curtis

9. U.S. Archives: Civil War and New Mexico conflict: Papers for James Perry Brantley, and Mark Brantley

10. U.S. RECORDS OF MEN ENLISTED IN THE U.S. ARMY:

    James Brantley, Joseph Brantley, Josiah Brantley Sr., John Brantley, Josiah Brantley Jr.

11. The United States of America Homestead Certificate: for Joel W. Curtis

12. United States Census Records: for the Brantley and Curtis family's

    Curtis: 1850 – Arkansas, Crawford, Marion County

    1870 – New Mexico, Colfax County, Raton

    1880 – New Mexico, Colfax County, Elizabeth City & Raton

    1900 New Mexico, Otero County, Weed Tws

    1900 – New Mexico, Colfax County, Raton, Cemelatio Tws, Blassburg P16, Springer

    1900 – Texas, Hansford County

    1910 – New Mexico, Otero County, Mayhill Tws

    1910 – New Mexico, Colfax County, Raton

    1920 – New Mexico, Taos County, Cordova City

    1920 – New Mexico, Grant County, Santa Rita Tws

    1920 – New Mexico, Colfax County, Raton

1920 – New Mexico, Chaves County, Roswell

Brantley:1830 – Illinios, Green County

1830 – Texas, Red River County

1835 – Illinios, Morgan County

1850 – Texas, Bastrop County

1850 – Texas, Red River County

1860 – Texas, Burnet County

1870 – Texas, Burnet County

13. The Library of Congress (A Century of Lawmaking for a New Nation: U.S. Congressional Documents and Debates 1774 – 1875)

   Journal of the—January 13, 1874, page 234 & House of Representatives February 1, 1869, page 241

14. Papers, Document, Photos, Letters, and all other: Curtis Family and Brantley Family: too many to list!

9 781438 900438